*Europe*

## Titles in this series

# *Europe*

## An Unfinished Adventure

# ZYGMUNT BAUMAN

polity

First published in 2004 by Polity Press

Polity Press
65 Bridge Street
Cambridge CB2 1UR, UK.

Polity Press
350 Main Street
Malden, MA 02148, USA

ISBN: 0-7456-3402-8
ISBN: 0-7456-3403-6 (paperback)

A catalogue record for this book is available from the
British Library

Typeset in 10.5 on 12 pt Plantin
by Kolam Information Services Pvt. Ltd, Pondicherry, India
Printed and bound in Great Britain by MPG Books Ltd,
Bodmin, Cornwall

For further information on Polity, visit our website:
www.polity.co.uk

# Contents

# *Acknowledgements*

I am grateful to Giuseppe Laterza and John Thompson for prevailing on me to develop a one-off text prepared for a lecture in Leyden into a wider survey of the current prospects of Europe struggling for unity, reason and ethical conscience in the increasingly fragmented world of passions and ethical confusion. It is thanks to them that I dared to take up the task, though flaws in its fulfilment are solely my responsibility.

My thanks go also, once more, to my editor Ann Bone, whose infinite patience proved to be in this case particularly precious due to the subject-matter that mutated faster than the writing managed to proceed . . .

# 1

## An Adventure called 'Europe'

When Princess Europa was kidnapped by Zeus in bull's disguise, her father, Agenor, King of Tyre, sent his sons in search of his lost daughter. One of them, Cadmon, sailed to Rhodes, landed in Thrace, and set out to explore the lands destined to assume later the name of his hapless sister. In Delphi he asked the Oracle about his sister's whereabouts. On that specific point Pythia, true to her habit, was evasive – but she obliged Cadmon with practical advice: 'You won't find her. Better get yourself a cow, follow it and push it forward, don't allow it to rest; at the spot where it falls from exhaustion, build a town.' This is, so the story goes, how Thebes was founded (and so – let us, wise after the fact, observe – a chain of events was started that served Euripides and Sophocles as the yarn out of which they wove the European idea of law, enabling Oedipus to practise what was to become the common frame for the character, torments and life dramas of the Europeans). 'To seek Europe', comments Denis de Rougemont on Cadmon's lesson, 'is to make it!' 'Europe exists through its search for the infinite – and this is what I call *adventure*.'[1]

Adventure? According to the *Oxford English Dictionary*, in Middle English that word meant anything that happened without design – a chance, hap, luck. It also meant a happening pregnant with danger or a threat of loss: risk, jeopardy; a hazardous enterprise or hapless performance. Later, closer to our own modern times, 'adventure' came to mean putting one's chances to the test: a venture, or experiment – a novel or exciting endeavour as yet untried. At the same time, a derivative was born: the *adventurer* – a highly ambivalent noun, whispering in one breath of blind fate and cunning, of craftiness and prudence, of aimlessness and determination. We may surmise that the shifts of meaning followed the maturation of the European spirit: its coming to terms with its own 'essence'.

The saga of Cadmon's travels, let us note, was not the only ancient story that sent such a message; far from it. In another tale, Phoenicians set sail to find the mythical continent and took possession of a geographic reality that was to become Europe. According to yet another story, after the deluge, when he divided the world between his three sons, Noah sent Japheth ('beauty' in Hebrew, by the way) to Europe, to follow there God's promise/command to be 'fruitful, and multiply: to bring forth abundantly in the earth, and multiply therein' (Genesis 9: 7). He equipped him with arms and emboldened him with a promise of infinite expansion: 'God shall enlarge Japheth' (Genesis 9: 27), 'dilatatio' according to the Vulgate and Fathers of the Church. The commentators of the biblical message point out that when instructing his sons Noah must have counted solely on Japheth's prowess and industry, since he equipped him with no other tool of success.

There is a common thread running through all the stories: Europe is not something you discover; Europe is a mission – something to be made, created, built. And it takes a lot of ingenuity, sense of purpose and hard labour to accomplish that mission. Perhaps a labour that never ends, a challenge always still to be met in full, a prospect forever outstanding.

Tales differed, but in all such tales Europe was invariably a site of adventure. Adventures like the interminable
travels undertaken to discover it, invent it or conjure it up;
travels like those which filled the life of Odysseus, who was
reluctant to return to the dull safety of his native Ithaca
since he was drawn by the excitement of untasted hazards
more than by the comforts of familiar routine, and who
was acclaimed (perhaps for that reason) as the precursor,
or the forefather, or the prototype, of the European. Europeans were the adventurers among the lovers of peace and
quiet: compulsive and indefatigable wanderers among the
shy and sedentary, ramblers and roamers among those
who would rather live their lives in a world ending at the
outermost village fence.

There is an old debate, as yet unresolved: was H. G.
Wells, inquisitive and insightful observer as he was, right
when he averred that 'in the country of the blind the one-
eyed man is king'? Or is it rather the case that in a country
of the blind a one-eyed man can only be a monster, a
sinister creature feared by all 'normal' countrymen?

In all probability, the debate will stay unresolved, since
the arguments on both sides are weighty and each is in its
own way persuasive. It needs to be pointed out, however,
that both antagonists in the debate assume an 'either-or'
where there is none. One possibility lost in their verbal
duel is an 'and-and' situation: the one-eyed man being a
king *as well as* an ogre (not a rare occurrence in past and
present history, to be sure). Loved *and* hated. Desired *and*
resented. Respected *and* reviled. An idol to be revered *and*
a fiend to be fought to the last ditch – on some occasions
simultaneously, at other times in quick succession. There
are situations in which the self-confident one-eyed king
may ignore or dismiss, unperturbed, the few monster-
baiting and busy detractors and prophets of doom crying
from wilderness. There are other times, however, when the

one-eyed monster would gladly abdicate his royal preten-
sions together with royal perks and duties, run for shelter
and shut the door behind him. But it may not be in the
one-eyed man's power, and surely not in his power only, to
choose between royalty and monstrosity – as the European
adventurer has learned, and is still learning to his baffle-
ment or despair, from his own stormy adventures.

More than two millennia have passed since Europe's
tales of origin, the Europe-originating tales, were com-
posed. The journey that started and went on as an adventure has left a thick and heavy deposit of pride and shame,
achievement and guilt; and it has lasted long enough for
the dreams and ambitions to gel into stereotypes, for the
stereotypes to freeze into 'essences', and for the essences to
ossify into 'facts of the matter' as hard as all facts of all
matters are assumed to be. Like all facts of the matter,
Europe is expected, in defiance of everything that made it
what it has become, to be a reality that could (should?) be
located, taken stock of and filed. In an age of territoriality
and territorial sovereignty, all realities are presumed to be
spatially defined and territorially fixed – and Europe is no
exception. Neither is the 'European character', nor the
'Europeans' themselves.

Alexander Wat, a notable avant-garde Polish poet who
was shuffled between the revolutionary barricades and the
gulags that spattered the continent of Europe in his lifetime and had ample opportunity to taste in full the sweet
dreams and the bitter awakenings of the past century –
notorious for its abundance of hopes and wretchedness of
frustrations – scanned the treasure boxes and rubbish bins
of his memory to crack the mystery of the 'European
character'. What would a 'typical European' be like? And
he answered: 'Delicate, sensitive, educated, one who won't
break his word, won't steal the last piece of bread from the
hungry and won't report on his inmates to the prison

guard . . . ' And then added, on reflection, 'I met one such man. He was an Armenian.'

You can quarrel with Wat's definition of 'the European' (after all, it is in the character of Europeans to be unsure of their true character, to disagree and endlessly quarrel about it), but you would hardly dispute, I suppose and hope, the two propositions implied by Wat's moral tale. First, the 'essence of Europe' tends to run ahead of the 'really existing Europe': it is the essence of 'being a European' to have an essence that always stays ahead of reality, and it is the essence of European realities to always lag behind the essence of Europe. Second, while the 'really existing Europe', that Europe of politicians, cartographers and all its appointed or self-appointed spokespeople, may be a geographical notion and a spatially confined entity, the 'essence' of Europe is neither the first nor the second. You are not necessarily a European just because you happen to be born or to live in a city marked on the political map of Europe. But you may be European even if you've never been to any of those cities.

Jorge Luis Borges, one of the most eminent among the great Europeans in any except the geographical sense, wrote of the 'perplexity' that cannot but arise whenever the 'absurd accidentality' of an identity tied down to a particular space and time is pondered, and so its closeness to a fiction rather than to anything we think of as 'reality' is inevitably revealed.[2] This may well be a universal feature of all identities traced down to the fact of heredity and belonging, but in the case of 'European identity' that feature, that 'absurd accidentality', is perhaps more blatant and perplexing than in most. Summing up the present-day confusion that haunts all attempts to pin down European identity, Alex Warleigh observed recently that the Europeans (in the sense of 'EU member-state nationals') 'tend to emphasize their diversity rather than what they have in common', whereas 'when talking of a "European" identity it is no longer possible to restrain its scope to EU member states in any analytically sound way.'[3] And as Norman Davies, a formidable historian, insists, it has been difficult at all times to decide where Europe begins and where it ends – geographically, culturally or ethnically. Nothing has changed in this respect now. The sole novelty is the fast rising number of standing and ad hoc committees, academic congresses and other public gatherings dedicated exclusively or almost to the squaring of this particular circle.

Whenever we hear the word 'Europe' spoken, it is not immediately clear to us whether it refers to the confined territorial reality, tied to the ground, within the borders fixed and meticulously drawn by as yet unrevoked political treaties and legal documents, or to the free-floating essence that knows no bounds and defies all spatial bonds and limits. And it is this difficulty, nay impossibility of speaking of Europe while separating clearly and neatly the issue of the essence and the facts of reality that sets the talk of Europe apart from most ordinary talk about entities with geographic references.

The vexing ethereality and stubborn extraterritoriality of the 'essence' saps and erodes the solid territoriality of European realities. Geographical Europe never had fixed borders, and is unlikely ever to acquire them as long as the 'essence' goes on being, as it has been thus far 'free-floating' and only loosely, if at all, tied to any particular plot in space. And whenever the states of Europe try to put their common 'continental' borders in place and hire heavily armed border guards and immigration and customs officers to keep them there, they can never manage to seal them, make them tight and impermeable. Any line circumscribing Europe will remain a challenge for the rest of the planet and a standing invitation to transgression.

Europe as an ideal (let us call it 'Europeanism') defies monopolistic ownership. It cannot be denied to the 'other', since it incorporates the phenomenon of 'otherness': in the practice of Europeanism, the perpetual effort to separate, expel and externalize is constantly thwarted by the drawing in, admission, accommodation and assimilation of the 'external'. Hans-Georg Gadamer considered it the 'particular advantage' of Europe: its ability 'to live with the others, to live as the other of the other', the capacity and necessity of 'learning to live with others even if the others were not like that'. 'We are all others, and we are all ourselves.' The European life is conducted in the constant presence and in the company of the others and the different, and the European way of life is a continuous negotiation that goes on despite the otherness and the difference dividing those engaged in, and by, the negotiation.[4]

It is perhaps because of such internalization of difference that marks Europe's condition that (as Krzysztof Pomian memorably put it) Europe came to be the birthplace of a *transgressive* civilization – a civilization of transgression (and vice versa!)[5] We may say that if it is measured by its horizons and ambitions (though not always by its deeds), this civilization, or this culture, was and remains a mode of life that is *allergic to borders* – indeed to all *fixity* and *finitude*. It suffers limits badly; it is as if it drew borders solely to target its intractable urge to trespass. It is an intrinsically expansive culture – a feature closely intertwined with the fact that Europe was a site of the sole social entity that in addition to *being* a civilization also *called itself* 'civilization' and looked at itself as civilization, that is as a product of choice, design and management – thereby recasting the totality of things, including itself, as an in-principle-unfinished object, an object of scrutiny, critique, and possibly remedial action. In its European rendition, 'civilization' (or 'culture', a concept difficult to separate from that of 'civilization' despite the philosophers' subtle arguments and the less subtle efforts of nationalist politicians) is a continuous process – forever imperfect yet obstinately struggling for perfection – of *remaking the world*. Even when the process is performed in the name of conservation, the hopeless inability of things to stay as they are, and their habit of successfully defying all undue tinkering unless they are duly tinkered with, is the common assumption of all conservation. It is viewed, including the conservatives, as a *job to be done*, and indeed that assumption is the prime reason to view that job as a job that needs doing.

Paraphrasing Hector Hugh Munro's (Saki's) witticism, we could say that the people of Europe made more history than they could consume locally. As far as history was concerned, Europe was definitely an exporting country, with (until quite recently) a consistently positive foreign trade balance . . .

To say that each human group has 'a culture' is banal, but it would not be banal to say it if it were not for Europe's discovery of culture as an activity performed by humans on the human world. It was that discovery which (to deploy Martin Heidegger's memorable terms) pulled the totality of the human world out of the dark expanses of *zuhanden* (that is 'given to hand' and given to hand matter-of-factly, routinely, and therefore 'unproblematically'), and transplanted it on to the brightly lit stage of *vorhanden* (that is, the realm of things that, in order to fit the hand, need to be watched, handled, tackled, kneaded, moulded, made different than they are). Unlike the universe of *zuhanden*, the world as *vorhanden* forbids standing still; it is a standing invitation, even a command, to act.

Once that discovery of the world-as-culture was made, it did not take long for it to become common knowledge. It was, we may say, a kind of knowledge singularly unfit for private ownership, let alone a monopoly, however hard the advocates and guardians of 'intellectual property rights' might try. The idea of culture stood after all for the discovery that *all things human are human-made* and that they would not be human things otherwise. This shared knowledge notwithstanding, the relations between European culture, the sole culture of self-discovery, and all the other cultures of the planet have been anything but symmetrical.

As Denis de Rougemont crisply put it,[6] Europe discovered all the lands of the earth, but no one ever discovered Europe. It dominated every continent in succession, but was never dominated by any. And it invented a civilization which the rest of the world tried to imitate or was forcefully compelled to replicate, but a reverse process never (thus far, at any rate) happened. These are all 'hard facts' of a history that has brought us, and the rest of the planet with us, to the place we all now share. One can define Europe, de Rougemont suggests, by its 'globalizing function'. Europe might have been, consistently and for a long time, an uncharacteristically adventurous corner of the globe – but the adventures on which it embarked in more than two millennia of its history 'proved to be decisive for the whole of humanity'. Indeed, just try to imagine the world with Europe absent from its history.

Goethe described the European culture as *Promethean*. Prometheus stole the fire of the gods and so betrayed the gods' secret to humans. Once wrenched from the hands of gods, fire was to be avidly sought by all and any human household and triumphantly kindled and kept aflame by those whose search was successful. Would it, however, have happened if not for Prometheus' cunning, arrogance and daring?

These crucial facts of history tend to be shamefacedly concealed nowadays, and recalling them is often attacked point blank in the name of the current version of 'political correctness'. What motivates the attackers?

Sometimes, undoubtedly, it is a sense of uneasiness caused by the facility with which any talk of Europe's unique qualities and historical role can be charged with the sin of 'Europocentrism'. This is a serious charge indeed, but it ought to be directed against the past European tendency to soliloquy when dialogue was in order; its preference for the teacher's authority and resentment of the learner's role; the notorious misuses of European military and economic superiority that marked its conspicuous, centuries-long presence in the world's history; against the high-handed treatment Europe accorded other forms of human life and its obliviousness to the wishes and voices of those who practised them; or against the atrocities committed under the cover of the civilizing mission – but not to a sober assessment of Europe's function as a yeast and moving spirit in the long, tortuous and still far from finished unification of planet-wide humanity.

There are reasons to suspect that on some other occasions the motive behind the denial of Europe's uniqueness is somewhat less noble – prompted by urges other than belated yet salutary modesty or repentance of guilt. One may surmise rather a conscious or more likely a *sub*conscious urge to wash our European hands of some unprepossessing consequences of Europe's endowment – of such qualities as were bound to make Europe into a factor in a 'planetary ferment' and an intrinsically expansive and expansible form of life (see for instance a recent intervention by Gøran Therborn[7]); a rather unflattering desire to avoid the onerous engagement with its duty towards the rest of humanity – a still outstanding duty, and a moral imperative more acute and compelling than ever in the past?

The shame of the adventurous past, or the ignominy of the explicit or implicit desire to draw a line under European adventure?

It was not just culture that happened to be Europe's discovery/invention. Europe also invented the need and the task of *culturing culture*.

Culture, let me repeat, is an incessant activity of drawing the world, fragment by fragment, out of the serene yet somnolent inertia of *zuhanden* and transplanting it into a uniquely human realm of *vorhanden* – making of the world an object of critical inquiry and creative action. This feat is accomplished ever anew, daily, everywhere where humans live; the perpetual rebirth and reincarnation of the world is what all and any human mode of being-in-the-world consists in.

Europe, though, went a step further than was common for the rest of humanity to go – and made that step before anyone else; though when taking that step it paved the way for all the others to follow. It committed the same *zuhanden–vorhanden* transfer on two tiers: it made culture itself the object of culture . . . First it was the 'world out there' which was transferred from the penumbra of *zuhanden* into the searchlight and spotlights of *vorhanden* – but thereafter the act of transfer itself was subjected to the same operation (as Hegel would say, that primary transfer was lifted from the modality of *an sich* to that of *für sich*). It was the human mode of being-in-the-world itself that was recast as a *vorhanden* object, as a problem to be tackled. Culture – the very process of the production of the human world – was made into an object of human theoretical and practical critique and of subsequent *cultivation*.

Europe was the first to proclaim that the 'world is made by culture' – but by the same token it was also the first to discover/decide that since culture is done by humans, doing culture is – may be, ought to be – a human *job/ destiny/vocation/task*. It was in Europe that humans first set themselves at a distance from their own mode of being-in-the-world and thereby gained autonomy from their own form of humanity. As Eduardo Lourenço, the Portuguese writer and resident, in succession, of Germany, Brazil and France, observed, European culture is perhaps for that reason a 'culture of uncertainty' – a 'culture of restlessness, of anguish and doubt',[8] a culture of radical defiance against all and any figures of certainty; and it could hardly be otherwise, since we *know* that culture is a kind of intellectual and spiritual practice that has *no foundation* except, as pointed out long ago by Plato, the dialogue that thought conducts with itself. But the outcome is that we, the Europeans, are perhaps the sole people who (as historical subjects and actors of culture) have *no identity* – fixed identity, or an identity deemed and believed to be fixed: 'we do not know who we are', and even less do we know what we can yet become and what we can yet learn that we are. The urge to *know* and/or to *become* what we are never subsides, and neither is the suspicion ever dispelled about what we may yet become following that urge. Europe's culture is one that knows no rest; it is a culture that feeds on questioning the order of things – and on questioning the fashion of questioning it.

Another kind of culture, a silent culture, a culture unaware of being a culture, a culture that keeps the knowledge of being a culture a secret, a culture working anonymously or under an assumed name, a culture stoutly denying its human origins and hiding behind the majestic edifice of a divine decree and heavenly tribunal, or signing an unconditional surrender to intractable and inscrutable laws of history – such a culture might be a handmaiden, a fuel station and a repair workshop servicing the current web of human interaction called 'society'. European culture is, however, anything but silent and self-denying – and for that reason it cannot but be a thorn in society's flesh, a spur to society's body, a pang of society's conscience. Day and night, it calls society to account and most of the time it keeps society on the defendants' bench. It will not take the 'is' as the answer to the 'ought' – let alone a clinching answer.

Europe trained itself in that role of a bespoke tailor to the human universe – practising the task on itself. But once having called the bluff of irrevocable verdicts of gods or nature and so having rendered the silence and self-denial of culture – any culture – no longer plausible, it also laid bare and made vulnerable every other part of the human universe, every other form of human togetherness and every other pattern of human interaction. As Paul Valéry observed at the start of the last century (at the time when Europe, at the zenith of its planetary rule, spotted or intuited the first contours of a downward slope on the other side of the mountain pass), the 'Europeanization' of the world reflected Europe's urge to *remake* the rest of the world, with no guilty conscience, according to European ends.

Remaking the world after the European pattern promised freedom of self-assertion to all, but at a price higher than most objects of the overhaul were willing to pay. From everyone they met on their worldwide travels, Europe's messengers demanded the ultimate sacrifice: surrender of the security that rested on monotonous self-reproduction. Brandishing Michel de Montaigne's injunction that 'we have no other criterion of truth or right-reason than the example and form of the opinions and customs of our own country',[9] Europe opened the way to tolerance of otherness, while declaring a war of attrition against every kind of otherness or sameness that failed or refused to try to rise to the standards it set. For Europe, the rest of the planet was not a source of *threats*, but a treasure house of *challenges*.

For many centuries, Europe was a keen exporter of its own surplus of history, inciting/forcing the rest of the planet to partake in its consumption. Those long centuries of one-sided, inequitable trade now rebound on Europe, facing it with the daunting task of consuming *locally* the surplus of *planetary* history.

From the start of the European adventure, but particularly during the most recent and vividly remembered, or at least most often recalled, centuries of its long history, the planet was, or at least seemed to be for Europe's restless, intrepid and adventurous spirits, Europe's playground. Those centuries were recorded in European history books as the 'age of geographic discoveries'. *European* discoveries, of course: by European envoys and emissaries, and for Europe's benefit.

Vast lands lay prostrated, waiting to be discovered. 'To discover' did not just mean to find and put on the sailors' maps. It meant to lay bare the treasures until then left idle, underused or misused, or put to all sorts of wrong, fanciful, unreasonable uses; treasures wasted on the natives ignorant of their value, lodes of riches clamouring to be mined – and then to harvest them and transfer them to other places where they could be turned to a better, sensible use. It also meant the opening up of immense yet deserted or sorely neglected spaces to human habitation and productive employment.

Europe needed/wanted both – the riches to replenish the depleted royal coffers, and the lands to accommodate men and women for whose physical survival or social ambitions there was not enough room at home. The earth was that vacuum which nature in its crowning, uppermost European incarnation abhorred and struggled to fill with bold, imaginative, businesslike, dogged and steadfast men who knew what was what and how to squeeze precious metals out of the base ore. And there were right people ready to fill the vacuum – huge, fast-growing masses of them.

Indeed, the more daring and exhilarating Europe's adventures grew at home, the more numerous were its collateral casualties. There were people who failed the ever more demanding tests of quality, adequacy and relevance, there were people declared ineligible for the test due to their inherent flaws, and people who refused to take the test because they did not care for the prizes promised to the successful, or feared to be disqualified whatever the results. Fortunately for the 'rejects' and those worrying how to dispose of them, there was an empty planet, or a planet that could be *made* empty, or could be viewed, treated and used *as if* it were empty. A planet with enough empty spaces on which Europe's problems (and most importantly, the 'problem people') could be dumped.

Now, at the end of the long day, it may well appear that the continuous need to dump them was one of the prime, perhaps even the principal moving force of Europe's planet-wide expansion – Europe's 'globalizing mission'.

For centuries, Europe felt itself to be the king of the planet and acted as such. Amidst the splendours of the royal court, the discomfort of being denounced as a monster and held up to reprobation could be played down as a minor and transient irritant and blamed on the obtuseness of the about-to-be beneficiaries of royal graces: their inability to appreciate the benefits which European rule was bound to lavish on the ruled in the fullness of time. Europe offered the superior way of life – better equipped, safer, richer, less hazardous and more dignified. It offered a vision of legal order that by comparison rendered all other (dis)orders akin to a jungle. European conquest was an ennobling act, elevating the conquered to the heights of true knowledge and higher morality. Or so, at least, Europe believed.

Except for a few niches difficult to penetrate, the whole of the planet has been remade after the European pattern; it either willingly accepted or reluctantly surrendered to the transgressive mode of existence which Europe embraced first and then spread to the furthest reaches of the globe. Towards the end of the twentieth century, Europe's mission had been accomplished – though not necessarily in the form and with the results that were dreamed of by the prophets and advocates of the 'civilized', human-friendly, peaceful, homely and hospitable world of Immanuel Kant's *allgemeine Vereinigung der Menschheit*, or the French *philosophes'* bright world of *Lumières*, of justice and equity, rule of law, reason and human solidarity. More than anything else, 'the really fulfilled mission' proved to be the global spread of a compulsive, obsessive and addictive urge for ordering and reordering (codename: modernization), and an irresistible pressure to downgrade and demote the past and current modes of living and of gaining a living by stripping them of their survival value and life-enhancing capacity (codename: economic progress): the two *spécialités de la maison européenne* responsible for the most prolific supply of 'human waste'.

Today the choice between the role of royalty and the plight of the monster seems to have fallen (or has it been torn?) out of the hands of the adventurer named Europe, and none of the stratagems it tested in its long career seems to be fit to get it back. On his visit to Poznań in 1997 Wolf Lepenies recited a lengthy list of reasons for Europe, that 'old continent in a young world' (as Goethe predicted it would inevitably become at the far end of its exciting and useful, yet timebound adventure), still so self-assured a short while ago, now to feel abashed, confused and ever more apprehensive.[10] Europe is getting grey-haired in a world that gets younger by the year: the demographers tell us that in the current decade the number of

Europeans under twenty years of age will fall by 11 per cent, while the number of those over sixty will grow by half. There will be, it seems, a smaller loaf to divide among a larger number of eaters.

The overall trend leaves little to the imagination: Germany, Great Britain and France, not so long ago the economic giants among dwarfs, are about to descend to respectively the tenth, nineteenth and twentieth places in the world ranking. They may well become NDCs (new *declining* countries) mark two, casualties of the exuberant growth and unstoppable rise of the NDCs mark one (new *developing* countries), and pushed by them, with ever more vigour, further down the ladder and further back to the tail of the pecking order. According to the prognosis of the International Monetary Fund, by 2010 three European countries among the richest Group of seven (Italy, Great Britain and France) will need to be replaced by other, younger economic powers if the changes in economic strength are to be reflected in the allotment of political honours.

And 'as the productive superiority of Europe deteriorates', concludes Lepenies, 'European ideas pale among other leading intellectual systems.' Little consolation can be found in the thought that the wondrous and spectacular transformation of the addressees and passive objects of the 'European mission' – until recently viewed as little more than supernumeraries in the play scripted and produced by Europe on the planetary stage – into brave, hard working and above all surprisingly talented and creative actors of the first rank may be the outcome of Europe's mission accomplished. Even if that transformation was, at least in part, a feat done *by* Europe, it did not turn out in the end to be done *for* Europe, and its beneficiaries neither admit to nor are recognized as being *of* Europe.

To its great distress and no less dismay, Europe discovers a possibility, indeed the likelihood, of 'modernization without Westernization' (read: without 'Europeanization'); a prospect of the self-appointed teachers being outrun and outperformed by their erstwhile pupils without their teachings having been gratefully acknowledged. In current literature, that mixture of perplexity and frustration has been dubbed the 'crisis of European identity'. 'We have lost', complains Lepenies, 'the will and the ability of long-distance orientation.' And 'having lost the capacity of long term thinking . . . European elites have ceased to offer an attractive example to follow.'

Another unanticipated, though retrospectively hardly unpredictable, consequence of the worldwide success of the European mission: the most recently 'Europeanized' parts of globe are confronted today with a phenomenon previously unknown to them – 'surplus population' and the problems of its disposal, and at a time when the planet is already full and no 'empty lands' are left to serve as waste-disposal sites. Neither neighbouring nor faraway lands are these days about to invite their surplus, nor will they be easily forced to accept it and accommodate it, as they themselves were in the past. The 'latecomers to (Europe-born) modernity' are left to stew in their own juice and to seek, desperately yet in vain, local solutions to globally caused problems.

Tribal wars and massacres, the proliferation of 'guerrilla armies' (often little more than bandit gangs in thin disguise) busy decimating each other's ranks yet in the process absorbing and annihilating the 'population surplus' (mostly prospectless youth, unemployable at home) are one of such 'local solutions to global problems' which the 'latecomers to modernity' tend to deploy. Hundreds of thousands of people are chased away from their homes, murdered, or forced to run for their lives away from their ravaged and devastated countries. Perhaps the most thriving industry in the lands of the latecomers (deviously and deceitfully dubbed 'developing countries') is the mass production of refugees. It is the ever more prolific product of that industry which the British prime minister, anticipating or echoing the sentiments prevailing in the rest of a startled and alarmed Europe, proposed recently to unload 'near their home countries', in permanently temporary camps (deviously and deceitfully dubbed 'safe havens'), in order to keep 'local problems' of local peoples local and so nip in the bud any attempts by latecomers to follow the example of the pioneers of modernity in seeking global (and the sole effective) solutions for locally manufactured problems.

However earnest, the efforts of European governments to stem and tightly control the tide of 'economic immigration' are not and probably cannot be made a hundred per cent successful. Protracted misery makes millions desperate, and in an era of globalized crime one can hardly expect there to be a shortage of criminal services eager to make a few or a few billion bucks through capitalizing on that desperation. Hence the millions of migrants wandering the routes once trodden by the 'surplus population' discharged by the European greenhouses of modernity – only in the reverse direction, and (at any rate thus far) unassisted by the armies of *conquistadores,* tradesmen and missionaries. The full dimensions of that consequence and its many repercussions are yet to unravel, to be absorbed, noticed and assessed.

For the time being, Europe and its overseas offspring/ outposts (like the United States or Australia) seem to look for an answer to their unfamiliar problems in similarly unfamiliar policies hardly ever practised in European history; policies inward- rather than outward-looking, centripetal rather than centrifugal, implosive rather than explosive – like retrenchment, falling back upon themselves, building fences equipped with a network of X-ray machines and closed circuit television cameras, putting more officials inside immigration booths and more border guards outside, tightening the nets of immigration and naturalization law, keeping refugees in closely guarded and isolated camps and stopping the others before they have a chance to claim refugee or asylum-seeker status – in short, sealing their own domains against the crowds knocking at the doors while doing pretty little, if anything at all, to relieve such pressure by removing its causes.

Naomi Klein noted an ever stronger and more widespread tendency (pioneered by the European Union but quickly followed by the US) towards a 'multi-tiered regional stronghold'.

> A fortress continent is a bloc of nations that joins forces to extract favourable trade terms from other countries, while patrolling their shared external borders to keep people from those countries out. But if a continent is serious about being a fortress, it also has to invite one or two poor countries within its walls, because somebody has to do the dirty work and heavy lifting.[11]

NAFTA, the US internal market extended to incorporate Canada and Mexico ('after oil,' Naomi Klein points out, 'immigrant labour is the fuel driving the southwest economy' of the US), was supplemented in July 2001 by 'Plan Sur', according to which the Mexican government took responsibility for the massive policing of its southern boundary to effectively stop the tide of impoverished human waste flowing to the US from Latin American countries. Since then, hundreds of thousands of migrants have been stopped, incarcerated and deported by Mexican police before reaching the US border. As for Fortress Europe, Naomi Klein suggests, 'Poland, Bulgaria, Hungary and the Czech Republic are the postmodern serfs, providing low-wage labour for the factories where clothes, electronics and cars are produced for 20–25 per cent of the cost of making them in Western Europe.' Inside fortress continents, 'a new social hierarchy' has been put in place in an attempt to strike a balance of sorts between blatantly contradictory, yet equally vital postulates: of airtight borders and of an easy access to cheap, undemanding, docile labour ready to accept and do whatever is on offer; or of free trade and of the need to pander to popular anti-immigrant sentiments – that straw clutched by governments in charge of the sinking sovereignty of nation-states. 'How do you stay open to business and closed to people?' asks Klein. And answers: 'Easy. First you expand the perimeter. Then you lock down.'

The funds which European Union transferred most willingly and with no haggling whatsoever to the East European and Central European countries applying for accession were those earmarked for the fortification of their eastern borders.

Somehow, the world 'out there' has stopped feeling to Europeans like a site of exciting adventure and invigorating challenge. No longer does the globe feel inviting and hospitable; neither does it look like an empty stage for countless heroic exploits and glorious unheard-of feats. It seems hostile and threatening now – bristling with all sorts of traps, ambushes and other unspeakable dangers for the unwary; full of lands seething with hatred, crowded with plotting and conspiring rogues – treacherous and villainous rascals, ready for any imaginable or unimaginable evildoing. 'We' won't go *there* (unless for a holiday – best of all to the beach hotels off-limits to all natives except barmen, waiters and maids). As to 'them' – they should be stopped from coming *here*.

'Created to assure free circulation inside the European Union, the "Schengen area" has become a formidable tool for controlling and recording the movements of its citizens', Jelle van Buuren discovers.[12] Among more than a million persons registered in the Schengen computers by 2001, 90 per cent consisted of 'undesirables'. Since then, things have progressed fast, boosted by the new conditions of security alert and semi-martial law. It is now planned to register a host of personal data about every man or woman entering the Schengen realm with a visa (the US, as usual, were the first here, deciding to fingerprint and photograph all visa-holding foreigners); if no exit is recorded in the allowed timespan, the culprit will be declared 'illegal', liable to be arrested and banished from Europe indefinitely. In a radical shift of purpose, never publicly discussed, the Council of Europe published a document on 6 November 2001 which pronounced that the 'Schengen system' was to serve 'to improve the internal security' of Europe's residents through a strict control of all comers. Coupled with the new stringent restrictions imposed on applications for asylum, the immediate result was (in the words of Amnesty International) 'an insult to those who have fled persecution, torture and possible death'.[13]

As soon became clear, while outsiders (refugees, bread-and-water or asylum seekers) might be denied some of their human rights, the burden of the new security regime would not spare the citizens of the European Union and its constituent states. In the name of security threatened by the hostility of the planet, measures unheard of almost since the times of Habeas Corpus have been introduced in one country after another to allow 'preventive' incarceration at secret police discretion and without trial, routine violation of privacy, access of secret services to the most intimate information related to any suspect – however tenuous or downright mistaken might be the reasons for suspicion.

It may (and should) be argued that on a planet viewed as hostile, insidious and guileful (barring a few enclaves currently seen as 'friendly'), defending democracy and personal freedom in one country taken on its own, or even in a federation of several countries enclosed behind the walls of a 'regional fortress', must be a daunting, perhaps impossible, task. *Defence of freedom has now become a global task –* and in its case, as in all other cases once dealt with locally but now entangled in anything but a local web of dependencies, solutions to globally gestated problems can only be global.

Time to return to our question: is the centuries-long European adventure running out of steam and grinding to a halt?

Wolf Lepenies seems to think so. At any rate, in the lecture already quoted he alerted his listeners to the fact that Europe has to a great extent lost its long-term orientation, complete with the will to resurrect and repossess it. He also warned that once deprived of the qualities that used to be its trademark, Europe ceased to be an attractive example for other inhabitants of the shared planet.

We may go a step further and note that the governments of Europe have lost vision, especially long-term vision, as distinct from the 'problem resolution' and 'crisis management' policies calculated for stretches of time that hardly ever reach beyond the next parliamentary election. Worse than that, Europe as a whole has lost its urge and will for adventure – for the excitement of risk-taking, for chasing new and unexplored horizons and blazing new and untried trails. This is, at least, the impression one gets when listening to the people whom the nations of Europe have elected to speak and act in their name. Reading through the text of the Maastricht Treaty – the document sketching the future of Europe and the target towards which half a billion Europeans are called to work – one would hardly be overwhelmed by 'constitutional patriotism' of the kind in which Jürgen Habermas discerns an emergent, detoxified version of national and community sentiments; or by any other strong feeling, for that matter, except tedium and ennui. If the Maastricht Treaty, or the Accession Treaty that followed it, is the contemporary equivalent of the Declaration of the Rights of Man and of the Citizen, the American Declaration of Independence or the Communist Manifesto, then there seems little hope left for the next instalment of the European adventure. More specifically, for Europe retaining its fate/vocation of being the global yeast of shared global history . . .

Promoting the 'Western way of life' as the superior pattern for everyone else to follow is no longer, as Couze Venn aptly observed, 'legitimated in terms of the humanist grand narratives of the Enlightenment'.[14] Indeed, 'the forces of new disciplinary power' try to sell the new 'world order' over which they preside in the name of efficiency, flexibility and marketization – terms which, we may add, acquire sinister meanings of insecurity, loss of livelihood, precariousness of existence, denial of dignity and cancellation of life prospects once they are translated into the native vernaculars away from the metropolis. 'The end of the Cold War/Third World War', Venn suggests, 'has released capitalism from needing to respond to calls for responsibility . . . It has lost the ability to respond to suffering.'

What does the West, as represented in the eyes of the planet by its self-appointed American leaders, offer the suffering part of the globe? A few examples drawn from the policies conducted in postwar Iraq (under the code-name of 'reconstruction') and collated most recently by Antonia Juhasz of the International Forum on Globalization[15] unravel the latent – yet palpably obvious to those on the receiving end – meaning of the current worldwide free-trade crusade. Let's leave aside – because they have been widely publicized and dismissed as the (unavoidable and arguably transient) side-effects of war – such direct consequences of the Western military intervention as 50–70 per cent unemployment, a sharp increase in maternal mortality as well as in the incidence of water-borne and vaccine-preventable diseases, and a doubling in the level of acute malnutrition, and focus instead on the way in which the postwar *reconstruction* of Iraq is intended to proceed under the auspices of 'Western efficiency-boosting market-ization'. The rebuilding of the water supply was commissioned from the Bechtel Corporation, even though water charges were tripled after a similar job done not long ago in Cochabamba, Bolivia, and families earning 60 dollars a month were treated to 20 dollar water bills once the local water supplies had been 'modernized' (popular riots followed, which forced the Bolivian government to cancel the contract – to which Bechtel responded with a 25 million dollar lawsuit). Another company, MCI, which was recently charged and found guilty of cheating when trading under its former name WorldCom, has been paid to construct the Iraqi wireless telephone network. Yet another company was commissioned to build, at a cost of 15 million dollars, a cement factory which was eventually constructed by an Iraqi businessman for 80,000 dollars. But Order 39 issued by the coalition-appointed Iraq governor Paul Bremer forbids the future native rulers of Iraq to 'restrict access by foreign owners to any sector of the economy', while it simultaneously authorizes foreign investors to 'transfer abroad without delay all funds associated with investment, including shares or profits and dividends'. One could excuse the natives for translating 'triumph of freedom and democracy' as syndicated robbery of resources and the promotion of an organized as well as officially endorsed corruption.

Alongside the Americans and the Japanese, Europeans are today the most zealous and indefatigable travellers: the count of miles per person per annum of Europeans probably dwarfs the scores that the natives of other continents can boast. But Europe is inward-looking. For most European globe-trotters, the rest of the world is no longer a mission; it is now a tourist haunt. Provided, of course, the service is swift and the servants are smiling, the en-suite facilities and bar supplies are in working order, the catering is of good quality, armed guards and closed-circuit TV cameras stand sentry – and the price is right.

Tourists seldom engage in lengthy exchanges with the natives. If they quarrel, it is mostly a bout of haggling about the price of market goods. The tourist–native relations are strictly on a service-for-money basis. The tourists meet the natives as buyers and sellers – smiling, yes, but nothing personal, you know . . . Transaction accomplished, we go, each of us, our own way. Trade is what brings us together, for as long as it takes to swap commodities for money, and let's leave the rest where it belongs, and where it should stay: in silence. What you and I have to offer each other has its market price. Once the market has spoken, there is nothing more to be said – and who are you and who am I to dispute the verdicts of the market?

Not all Europeans (like the Americans) travel the world as tourists. Some come to the distant places to sell products. In the case of a few of them, those in the diplomatic service or on another official mission, the 'product' they 'sell' is their own country or continent, and what they are after is their right, and the right of those for whom they act as spokespersons, to go on viewing and treating the rest of the planet as a collection of tourist haunts and trading outposts. Naomi Klein describes the experience of one of such travelling salespeople, Charlotte Beers, the Under Secretary of State for Public Diplomacy and Public Affairs (so not a first generation European, yet not that distant from European ways either), charged by the US administration with the task of 'overhauling the US image abroad':

> when Beers went on a mission to Egypt in January [2002] to improve the image of the US among Arab 'opinion makers', it didn't go well. Muhammad Abdel Hadi, an editor of the newspaper *Al Ahram*, left his meeting with Beers frustrated that she seems more interested in talking about vague American values than about specific US policies. 'No matter how hard you try to make them understand,' he said, 'they don't.'[16]

Klein refers to US unilateralism in the face of international laws, to its initiation or promotion of the widening wealth disparities, to the crackdown on immigrants, and to human rights violations – to conclude that 'America's problem is not with its brand . . . but with its product.' 'If they [the natives bearing the brunt of such policies] are angry, as millions clearly are, it's because they have seen the promises betrayed by US policy.' What 'they' see and take note of are not only the comfortable Nike sneakers and seductive Barbie dolls that it is hoped will play roving ambassadors for American (Western) values and the joys that freedom and democracy may bring you. 'They' know, from their own experience, that the 'travels of Nike sneakers' can be 'traced back to the abusive sweatshops of Vietnam, Barbie's little outfits to the child labour of Sumatra' – and that some multinationals, confident of the support and protection of the smart missiles ready to promote American (and Western) values where they are not welcome, 'far from levelling the global field with jobs and technology for all, are in the process of mining the planet's poorest . . . for unimaginable profits'.[17]

Few people on earth could possibly have failed to hear the message of freedom or democracy, repeated on every occasion and without occasion. If, however, those many who heard the message try to unpack its contents by watching the conduct of its senders, they may be excused for reading selfishness, cupidity, greed and the precept of each man for himself and the devil take the hindmost into 'freedom', and 'might is right' into 'democracy'. They can be forgiven for looking askance at the messages or their senders whom they suspect of bearing responsibility for the deception.

With a modicum of good will, one can understand why such people insist on a translation that refutes the manifest contents of the message. What they know all too well from their daily experience is that the surrender to the rule of planetary markets which has been proclaimed to be the condition of freedom and democracy, to the cut-throat competition which that rule puts in the place of neighbourly cooperation and assistance, and to the massive privatization and deregulation that follow will deprive them of workplaces, farms, homes and communities, while giving little in exchange: not nearly enough schools or hospitals, no electricity or drinking water, and above all no human dignity and no prospects of a better life in their lifetime. Thus far the markets' bids for global domination, to quote Naomi Klein one last time,

> have bred armies of locked-out people, whose services are no longer needed, whose lifestyles are written off as 'backward', whose basic needs go unmet. [The] fences of social exclusion can discard an entire industry, and they can also

write off an entire country, as happened to Argentina. In the case of Africa, essentially an entire continent can find itself exiled to the global shadow world, off the map and off the news, appearing only during wartime when its citizens are looked on with suspicion as potential militia members, would-be terrorists or anti-American fanatics.[18]

There is, as one would expect, a reaction to this action and to its planned or inadvertent, ostensible or hushed-up consequences. Ryszard Kapuściński notes a profound change in the mood of the planet, surreptitious, subterranean and hardly ever or never noticed by travelling business people, itinerant craftworkers of knowledge or tourists comfortably enclosed in the cosy cocoons of customized nowherevilles – but a departure that would nevertheless appear seminal and full of foreboding once it was noted and scrutinized, particularly through European eyes.[19]

In the course of the last five centuries the well-nigh universal mentality of the globe developed in the shadow of the patterns, values and criteria identified with European culture. The military and economic domination of Europe was topped by the unchallenged position of Europe as the reference point for the evaluation, praise or condemnation of any other form of human life, past and present, and as the supreme court of law where such an assessment was authoritatively pronounced with no right of appeal. It was enough just to be a European, says Kapuściński, to feel like a boss and a ruler everywhere else. Even a mediocre person of humble standing and held in low esteem in his own small and insignificant (but European!) country rose to the highest social positions once he had landed in Malaysia or Zambia . . . This is no longer a case, though, as Kapuściñski has recently found. The present time is marked by an ever more blatant and outspoken self-awareness among the peoples who still half a century ago genuflected to a Europe perched on the altar of cargo cults. Now they show a fast-growing sense of their own value and an ever more evident ambition to gain and retain an independent and weighty place of their own in the new, increasingly egalitarian and multicultural world. Once upon a time, remembers Kapuściński, everyone in distant lands asked him about Europe, but these days no one does: today the 'natives' have their own tasks and problems clamouring for (and receiving) their, and all their, attention. 'The European presence' is ever less visible: physically as much as spiritually.

Casting the victims of the rampant globalization of the financial and commodity markets as first and foremost a security threat, rather than as people needing aid and entitled to compensation for the damage to their lives, has its obvious uses. It calms the scruples, and puts paid to ethical compunctions. One is, after all, dealing here with enemies who 'hate our values' and cannot bear the sight of us, ordinary folk like us, for our determination to live in freedom and democracy. It helps to divert the funds that could be used to narrow the disparities and defuse the animosities they spawn so to beef up the weapons industry, arms sales and stockholders profits, and so improve the statistics of home employment and raise the feel-good gradient of the home constituency. Last but not least, it whips up the flagging consumerist economy by condensing diffuse security fears and then retargeting and channelling them away from trouble and into the urge to buy little private fortresses on wheels (like the gas-guzzling yet pricey 'Hummers' or 'Sport Utility Vehicles', notoriously dangerous for the drivers and pedestrians alike); or by allowing the forceful promotion of lucrative 'brand rights' or 'intellectual rights' under the pretext of preventing the profits drawn from their violation from being shifted to terrorist cells.

Casting the victims of aggrandizement as first and foremost a security threat also allows the shedding of the irritating constraints of democratic control imposed or threatening to be imposed on business pursuits – by recasting political (and in the last account eminently economic) choices as military necessities. Here as elsewhere America takes the lead, though its moves are closely watched and eagerly followed by a large number of European governments. As William J. Bennett recently stated in a book aptly titled *Why We Fight: Moral Clarity and the War on Terrorism*,

> the threats we face today are both external and internal: external in that there are groups and states that want to attack United States: internal in that there are those who are attempting to use this opportunity to promulgate the agenda of 'blame America first'. Both threats stem from either a hatred for the American ideals of freedom and equality or a misunderstanding of those ideals and their practice.[20]

Bennett's credo can best be understood as an ideological gloss over a practice already in full swing – like the recently introduced 'USA Patriot Act', aimed explicitly at people engaged in the kind of political action heretofore protected by the American constitution – and legalizing heretofore prohibited clandestine surveillance, searches without warrants and other invasions of privacy, as well as incarceration without charge and trials of civilians before military courts.

Security services, like any other bureaucracy, are subject to the inexorable logic of the Parkinson's Law, or a self-fulfilling prophecy. Once set in place, they develop their own momentum, creating ever new targets on which to practise the arts they are best at practising, while recasting the rest of their field of action as a vast matrix of future targets. No wonder 'the West' – Europe and its globally scattered offspring – is increasingly inward-looking. The world looks and feels ever less inviting. It appears to be a hostile world, a treacherous, vengeance-breathing world, a world that still needs to be made safe for the Westerners-turned-tourists-and-trades people. It looks uncannily and eerily like a battlefield getting ready for an imminent 'war of civilizations'. It is a world in which all steps are fraught with danger, and so those daring enough to risk them must look out, stay constantly on the alert, and most crucially ought to stick to the places reserved for their sole and secure use and to the marked and protected tracks that connect them: tracks barbed-wired off from that wilderness spattered with ambushes for the unwary. Whoever forgets those precepts does it at her or his own risk and must be ready to bear the consequences.

In an insecure world, security is the name of the game, the game's main purpose and its paramount stake.

Security is a value that, in practice if not in theory, dwarfs and elbows out all other values, including those values proclaimed to be 'the dearest to us', being for that reason the prime targets of 'their' hatred, and the prime cause of 'their' wish, the wish of 'those out there', to harm us – the urge which makes the whole world, as well as this part 'in here' that we call our home, insecure. In a world as insecure as ours, all those things we used to associate with democracy, like personal freedom of speech and action, the right to privacy, access to truth, may clash with the supreme need for security and must therefore be trimmed or suspended. At least this is what the official version of the fight-for-security insists on and what official government practice implies.

The truth which fell as the first casualty of the form taken by the post-11 September security concerns is that we cannot effectively defend our freedoms here at home while fencing ourselves off from the rest of the world and attending solely to our own affairs.

There are valid reasons to suppose that on a globalized planet, where the plight of everyone everywhere determines and is determined by the plights of all others, one can no longer have freedom and democracy in one country, or only in a few selected countries. The fate of freedom and democracy in each land is decided and settled on the global stage – and only on that stage can it be defended with a realistic chance of lasting success. It is no longer in the power of any state, however heavily armed, resolute and uncompromising, to defend chosen values at home while turning its back on the dreams and yearnings of those outside its borders.

But turning our backs is precisely what we, Europeans and European descendants settled in Europe's erstwhile overseas colonies, do. Attuned to the rules of democracy locked (at its peril) in the borders of a nation-state or a combination of nation-states, we keep our riches and multiply them at the expense of the poor outside. As Joseph Stiglitz recently reminded the trade ministers preparing for their Cancún meeting, the average European subsidy per cow 'matches the 2 dollars per day poverty level on which billions of people barely subsist' – whereas America's 4 billion dollars worth of cotton subsidies paid to 25,000 well-off farmers 'bring misery to 10 million African farmers and more than offset the US's miserly aid to some of the affected countries'.[21] One occasionally hears Europe and America publicly accusing each other of 'unfair agricultural practices'. But, Stiglitz observes, 'neither side seems to be willing to make major concessions', whereas nothing short of major, radical concessions would convince others to stop looking at the unashamed display of 'brute economic power by the US and Europe' as

anything but an effort to defend the privileges of the privileged, to protect the wealth of the wealthy, and to serve
their own interests that boil down to more wealth and yet
more wealth. At the Cancún conference, which was meant
to create a joint platform on which the rich and the poor
could meet and exchange their products with mutual
benefit, the Senegalese trade minister Alchaton Agne
Poyue concluded, after the lengthy yet barren debate,
that the other, affluent side at the negotiation table did
not wish to nor did pay attention to 'our survival interest,
not to mention our "development" '. Meanwhile the en-
semble of sub-Saharan representatives, the part of the
world most affected by huge subsidies poured into American cotton farming, had just one name for the final declaration that promised future consultations about the thorny
issue of subsidies, while in the meantime advising the poor
countries 'to diversify their economies' (that is, to keep
away from cotton farming): an insult.[22]

And so, for the third time, let me ask the question: has its
historic time run out for the European adventure? For
Europe *as* adventure?

One can argue – forcefully and convincingly – that never
before has Europe needed to be as adventurous as it needs
to be now. And that never before has this planet, which the
millions of privileged and well-off Europeans share with
the poor and disadvantaged billions, needed an adventurous Europe as much as it needs it now: a Europe looking
beyond its frontiers, a Europe critical of its own narrow-
mindedness and self-referentiality, a Europe struggling to
reach out of its territorial confinement, with an urge to
transcend its own and by the same token the rest of the
world's condition; a Europe *with a planetary mission to
perform*. And perhaps differently from the past, when the
harvest of the European addiction to transgression was

anything but an unalloyed blessing for Europe's close and remote neighbours, and when the direct and collateral casualties of the European urge to transgress were thick on the planetary ground – this time the interests of Europe and of the peoples outside its borders will *not just coincide, but overlap*. It is enough for eyes to be raised a few inches higher than the level of momentary interests and crisis-management emergencies to see that for all practical intents and purposes these interests are closely inter-twined, if not identical.

In a speech to the European Parliament on 8 March 1994 Vaclav Havel, then President of the Czech Republic, suggested that Europe needs a Charter which would spell out what it means to be Europe, or to be European: a 'Charter of European identity' for the coming era of a planet struggling to take charge of its own imminent and inescapable unification. A manifesto, we may say, of Europe's raison d'être in the era of globalization.

One of the groups that followed Havel's call was the Europa-Union Deutschland, and the result was 'A Charter of European Identity' approved on 28 October 1995 at the Union's 41st Congress held in Lübeck.[23] Right after a predictable preamble dedicated to 'Europe as a community of destiny', two sections follow that deserve special attention. One speaks of 'Europe as a community of values' and names tolerance, humanity and fraternity as the foremost values which Europe 'spread throughout the world', becoming thereby 'the mother of revolutions in the modern world'. The authors of the Charter admit that in its long history Europe 'has repeatedly called these values into question and offended against them', but believe that now, at long last, after an age of 'unrestrained nation-alism, imperialism and totalitarianism', those values rooted in classical antiquity and Christianity have helped Europe to establish 'freedom, justice and democracy as the principles for international relations'. Another chapter presents Europe as 'a community of responsibility'. It points out that 'in today's world, in which we have all become interdependent, the European Union carries a particular responsibility' towards the rest of the world and that 'only through cooperation, solidarity and unity can Europe effectively help to solve world problems'. The European Union 'should set an example, in particular in relation to upholding human rights and the protection of minorities'. (One is tempted to add, though: also in relation to the protection of the huge majority of humankind against the consequences of the privileges enjoyed by a small minority of the planet's population, Europe included . . .)

Reading the Charter, one muses: easier said than done. The 'Charter of European Identity' is, blatantly, a utopian blueprint!

Such a verdict may well be correct – but then 'European identity' was a utopia at all moments in its history. Perhaps the sole steady element that made of European history a consistent and in the end cohesive story was the utopian spirit endemic to its identity, a forever not-yet-attained identity, vexingly elusive and always at odds with the realities of the day. Europe's place was at all times somewhere between the 'ought' and the 'is', and that is why it had to be, and indeed was, a site of continuous experimentation and adventure. Its present place is no different: it oscillates between the 'ought' of a hospitable, user-friendly planet determined to attain and secure a sustainable life for all its residents, and a planet of deepening disparities, tribal animosities and intertribal fences, a planet ever less fit for human habitation.

The ongoing institutional unification of Europe may be seen as (and prove to be) a defensive move prompted by the impulse to defend Europe's 'is' (its relatively peaceful niche amidst deepening planetary turmoil, its privileged life standards amidst worldwide deprivation) against the 'ought' of its challenging, uncomfortable yet imperative planetary responsibilities. But it may also prove to be a preliminary step towards taking up those responsibilities: a sensible attempt to gather resources, force and will, all necessary to tackle the tasks of supracontinental, planetary dimensions.

As Jürgen Habermas observed in one of his recent analyses,

> A nation state is not going to regain its old strength by retreating into its shell . . . A politics of self-liquidation – letting the state simply merge into postnational networks – is just as unconvincing. And postmodern neoliberalism cannot explain how the deficits in steering competences and legitimation that emerge at the national level can be compensated at the supranational level without new forms of political regulation . . . The artificial conditions in which national consciousness arose argue against the defeatist assumption that a form of civic solidarity among strangers can only be generated within the confines of the nation. If this form of collective identity was due to a highly abstractive leap from the local and dynastic to national and then to democratic consciousness, why shouldn't this learning process be able to continue?[24]

Another leap, similar to that accomplished by Europe at the threshold of modern times, in another turbulent era, is the imperative of the present generations. It points this time towards the space in which survival struggles are nowadays waged and in which the fate of all parts of the globe is decided: the politically empty and ethically confused planetary space lacking in 'steering competences' and legitimate legal and political authorities, and plagued by an awesome 'democratic deficit'.

Then, two to three hundred years ago, when negotiating that other 'mountain pass' (to use Reinhard Kosseleck's apt term), Europe invented *nations*. Now the point is to invent *humanity*. And there are no other actors in sight able and willing to attempt that last, ultimate act of transcendence in the long, tormented road of humanity towards itself – towards that *allgemeine Vereinigung der Menschheit* that two centuries ago was prophesied by Kant as its final destination not just by choice, but by 'Nature's verdict and design'.

Paradoxically, the chance to extend the European adventure into realms never visited before and perhaps even off-limits to Europe in its past king/monster phase arises at a time when Europe's specific gravity in the world affairs has fallen and seems to go on falling.

Paradoxically? Perhaps not paradoxically after all. Karl Deutsch famously defined power as 'the ability to afford not to learn'. Well, by this definition Europe has lost much of its power, as it has been denied the luxury of not-learning. Nowadays, Europe must learn – and it does. And while learning, it accumulates a constantly growing capital of life-saving knowledge that it may share with others: those who need such knowledge to afford what can still be afforded by Europe; and also, perhaps more importantly, those who can still afford what Europe definitely can no longer afford.

Its convoluted history led Europe to the point when it can hardly stop learning and memorizing the lesson. Its present, after all, is nothing if not the life of its memory. Europe's history shaped its adventurous character, while the forms the European adventure assumed in the past, by foreclosing certain options if not by opening new and obvious ones, supply the programme for its future avatars.

As two prominent Russian politologists, Vladislav Ino-zemtsev and Ekaterina Kuznetsova, point out, Europe 'could not adopt American rules without betraying its own postwar achievements'.[25] The salutary alternative which Europe – and only Europe – can offer, is based on the European – and only European – tradition. At a time when America, which relegated Europe to the second division of power games, has (in Will Hutton's words) 'disqualified itself from the fight for security, prosperity, and justice',[26] Europe, as Inozemtsev and Kuznetsova point out, having learned the truth the hard way, stoutly refuses 'to regard force as a source of justice', and even more so to confuse the two, and it is well placed to 'oppose the United States as *justice* opposes *force* rather than as *weakness* opposes *power*'.

Europe's pyromaniac past may be a sound reason for a lot of soul-searching and feelings of guilt, but singed fingers may yet prove an asset. They would be reluctant to play with fire – and averse to piling up powder kegs. 'The "old" Europe that has become wise should not become tired of showing this insight to its American friends', suggests Ulrich K. Preuss, referring to the European discovery that 'law creates trust, predictability, security; law enables', and to the bitter lesson that the 'overextension of their rule', that is 'rejecting law as a source for validity in order to rely on violence alone' and an inability to understand 'the world around them' as a result of resorting to the 'non-communicative violence of the military' as their sole guide, was the principal cause of the decline 'of virtually all empires in world history'.[27]

And so, to quote the trenchant Robert Kagan's statement, 'it is time to stop pretending that Europeans and Americans share a common view of the world, or even that they occupy the same world.'[28] The United States, Kagan suggests, 'remains mired in history, exercising power in the anarchic Hobbesian world', while Europe is already moving (though, let us observe, half-heartedly and not without many a hiccup, much back-pedalling and many second thoughts) towards the Kantian world of perpetual peace, in which law, negotiation and cooperation gain the upper hand where violence and raw force once ruled.

Europe is well prepared if not to *lead*, then most certainly to *show* the way from the Hobbesian planet to the Kantian 'universal unification of the human species'. It has traversed that road itself, at least the initial part of it, up to the station of 'peaceful neighbourly cohabitation', and knows only too well the human costs of deviations and delays. And for the last half-century it has put in practice, even if with only mixed success, the measures that need to be taken if any further advance on that road is to be achieved.

Étienne Balibar writes of 'the lesson of tragedy' that Europe finally learned.[29] Indeed, after hundreds of years of massive blood-lettings, whether talked of in religious, ethnic, tribal, racist or class terms – of the holy and unholy crusades that in retrospect look uncannily like fratricides every bit as iniquitous, unlofty and unheroic as they were cruel and ferocious and that could be dismissed as the mere teething troubles of immature, inchoate and still irrational humanity were not the devastation they left behind so enormous and so appalling in its inhumanity – came the moment of awakening and sobering up, ushering Europe into an as yet unfinished era of experimentation with what Balibar (after Monique Chemillier-Gendreau) names 'transnational public order': a kind of setting in which Clausewitz's rule no longer binds and wars are neither natural, nor permissible extensions of political action.

What endows Europe's apparently internal concerns and *domestic* exertions with particular significance for the emergent *planetary* order is however the dawning recognition of the truth brought home by the ever more blatant globality of human interdependence: that resistance to violence is bound to remain ineffective and simply won't do if it is limited to the 'metropolitan' framework. Two learning processes mentioned by Balibar converged on that truth.

First, the 'growing consciousness of the realities of colonial history'. Europe used to divide the world into the realms of 'civilization' and 'barbarism', little aware and/or reluctant to admit what it begins to accept now – that 'the greatest barbarity certainly was not on the side we imagined', even if resorting to violence and inhumanity was not only the conquerors' idiosyncratic predilection.

Second, Europe's long involvement with the rest of the human planet, the ubiquitous and obtrusive European presence in virtually every corner of the globe, however distant, has reverberated in 'a powerful, irreversible process of hybridization and multiculturalism now transforming Europe' that 'leads Europe to recognize, albeit with considerable hesitations and setbacks, that the other is a necessary component of its "identity" '.

The two learning processes have brought (or at least are bringing) Europe to a point where 'combining the different resources for institutionalizing conflicts' and 'progressively introducing new basic rights' (or, to use Amartya Sen's terminology, new 'capabilities') are likely to become a widely accepted imperative – a new way of living together and living with each other's differences, set to replace the violent trials of force and put paid to the war option. This prospect has been portrayed by Eugen Weber as the task 'to meld the scores of local fatherlands and cultures into one large, abstract entity'[30] – a feat already performed once in/by Europe in the era of nation-state building, but now looming large again on the immediate agenda, though this time with the added challenge of the much more formidable, planetary scale. The prospect is anything but a foregone conclusion. The fact of the matter is that when 'inflated to universal proportions, compassion falters. Solidarity on a national scale had been a hard row to hoe; it took time to inculcate. World solidarity proves a slacker bond still.'

The redoubtable counter-odds notwithstanding, trying hard to make that prospect real is still a must. Forging a frame able to accommodate the variety of human forms of life and induce those forms to engage in peaceful inter-action, cooperative in spirit and mutually beneficial, is a matter of life and death for everyone involved – for the presently deprived and the presently privileged alike. And it so happens that thanks to its unique history Europe is better placed than any other sector of humanity to rise to such a challenge and to insist, convincingly and effectively, that when it comes to a mode of living together on a planet transformed into a dense network of mutual dependency there is indeed *no viable nor plausible alternative*, since the security and well-being of one part of the globe can no longer be achieved, let alone guaranteed, unless the right to a secure and dignified life is extended to all, both in letter and in deed.

Robert Fine has recently discussed that prospect in reference to the emergent frame of mind (not unexpect-edly, spreading most buoyantly in Europe) that he chose to call 'the new or actually existing cosmopolitanism'.

> It is a way of thinking that declares its opposition to all forms of ethnic nationalism and religious fundamentalism as well as to the economic imperatives of global capitalism. It perceives the integrity of contemporary political life as threatened both by globalization of markets and by regres-sive forms of revolt against globalization, and aims to

reconstruct political life on the basis of an enlightened
vision of peaceful relations between nation states, human
rights shared by all world citizens, and a global legal order
buttressed by a global civil society.[31]

The above description, Fine hastens to add, refers in
equal measure to a 'theoretical approach toward understanding the world', 'a diagnosis of the age in which we
live', and 'a normative stance in favour of universalistic
standards of moral judgments, international law and political action'. All three, let us observe, have their roots
deeply sunk in the European experience and the also
European interpretation and exposition of its meaning.

As the great liberal thinker Richard Rorty suggests, 'the
Marxists were right about at least one thing: the central
political questions are those about the relations between
rich and poor.'[32] And yet 'we now have a global overclass
which makes all the major economic decisions, and makes
them in entire independence of the legislatures, and *a
fortiori* of the will of the voters, of any given country.'
'The absence of a global polity means that the super-rich
can operate without any thought of any interests save their
own.' But also, let me add, that absence means that the
'super-rich' operate with little or no chance of effective
opposition that would allow them to avoid defining their
'own interests' so narrowly as to make their actions sui-
cidal in addition to being insensitive, cruel, and occasionally murderous.

This is not only the question of the unsustainable polar-
ization of current and prospective living conditions, with
its incalculable yet potentially disastrous effects on the
security and dignity of human lives. Given the flat refusal
of the privileged part of humankind to mitigate the un-
scrupulous looting and burning out of the planet's energy

resources, it is the bare *survival of human species* that is now at stake. In the words of George Monbiot, summing up the consensual wisdom of expert climatologists,

> we are not contemplating the end of holidays in Seville. We are contemplating the end of the circumstances which permit most human beings to remain on Earth . . . In other words, if we leave the market to govern our politics, we are finished. Only if we take control of our economic lives, and demand and create the means by which we may cut our energy use to 10% or 20% of current levels will we prevent the catastrophe that our rational selves can comprehend.[33]

Wolf Lepenies summed up his Poznań lecture by calling 'for another Marx', who instead of *Capital: A Critique of Political Economy* would write a book called *Financial Markets: A Critique of Depoliticized Economy*. On the repoliticization of the economy, Lepenies insisted, depends the survival of democracy. In all probability, we may add, it is not only the survival of democracy, but also the continuing existence of the species that created it and found it good, that depends on that leap – on the 'Great Transformation Mark Two' that needs to follow the original Great Transformation initiated by Europe several centuries ago.[34]

The end of history is a myth – or an avoidable catastrophe. And so is the end of the European adventure – of Europe as adventure.

# 2

## *In the Empire's Shadow*

One art that Europe never had the occasion to learn since it became aware of being Europe (that is, since it set its ambitions as standards which were to be obeyed by its own practice and which all others were to be persuaded to adopt) was that of living in the shadow of a power mightier than itself, more ambitious and resourceful in its resolve to set its own ambitions as standards for everyone else's practice, and so also of holding such imported/imposed standards up to its own practice as the pattern to follow. Europe had never faced the threat of being conquered by another continent – and never before had it been looked at from on high and denigrated as a second-rate power obliged to swear allegiance to a foreign empire and ingratiate itself to an alien force it had little hope of mitigating, pacifying, or converting to its own ways – let alone of subduing it and subordinating it to its will. Never had Europe lived with a demeaning awareness of its own inferiority and with the experience of being obliged to look up to patterns of life preached and practised by others, of struggling to adjust and adapt its own acts to such patterns, of emulating alien forms of life and/or matching them by raising its forms of life to their level. Among Europe's numerous acquired abilities, the skills demanded by such contingencies were conspicuously missing.

A situation that demands such skills took Europe unprepared by its past history and its past conception of the global order as a *pax europeana* and of humanity as the end-product of the progressive universalization of the European mode of being. When Donald Rumsfeld, the US Secretary for Defense, speaks disdainfully of 'old Europe' (implying a Europe that has outlived its time, a Europe that is out of date and lagging behind, an antiquated and obsolete Europe, a fossil of bygone times), the object of his irony and derision is a Europe clinging to memories of past glories, still wishing to play first violin and refusing to accept second fiddle, and deluding itself that it is still capable of briefing the pipers and setting their tunes.

In their short and sharp analysis (quoted above) of the clash between 'European values' (read: Europe's historically formed and entrenched preferences and criteria of judgement) and 'American interests', Vladislav Inozemtsev and Ekaterina Kuznetsova cite a few authoritative or influential opinions that articulate the unspoken premises of Rumsfeld's verdict. 'America stands supreme in the four decisive domains of global power: militarily, economically . . . technologically, and culturally . . . It is the combination of all four that makes America the only comprehensive global superpower,' writes Zbigniew Brzezinski.[1] Henry Kissinger ventures a step further: 'At the dawn of the new millennium, the United States is enjoying a pre-eminence unrivalled by even the greatest empires of the past.'[2] Joseph S. Nye Jr chimes in: 'Not since Rome has one nation loomed so large above the other.'[3] In his widely debated study, Robert Kagan endorses that view: 'By historical standards, America's post-Cold War military power, particularly its ability to project that power to all corners of the globe, remains unprecedented.'[4]

Just as the sunset of European hegemony took Europe by surprise, the sudden elevation of the United States to the position of sole superpower and uncontested (at least not *realistically* contested) worldwide hegemony took American political leaders and opinion-makers unprepared. One would not expect rational, thought-through and carefully weighed strategic responses to a sudden and unanticipated change of fortune to be worked out overnight; an erratic and inconsistent string of confused and confusing fits and starts, 'gut reactions', ad hoc improvisations and hazardous gambles is likely to follow the trauma. It is therefore too early to pronounce on the nature of the new American empire, to generalize on its strategy and its impact on the state of the planet, and even less timely to prognosticate its future twists and turns and the form in which it will, if at all, ultimately settle. For the time being, the behaviour of the new empire is a major, arguably *the* major, factor of that uncertainty which was first (just at the time when the US found itself alone on a battlefield deserted by the counter-superpower) encapsulated in the notion of the 'New World Disorder' by Kenneth Jowitt, and more recently Tzvetan Todorov.

Michael Mann grasps the mood in which such behaviour is perceived by those who find themselves living in an imperial playground – that is all over the baffled planet. America, he says, is seen as 'a disturbed, misshapen monster stumbling clumsily across the world. It means well. It intends to spread order and benevolence, but instead it creates more disorder and violence.'[5] One could perhaps catch the current mixture of apprehension and bewilderment even better by resorting to the simile of 'an elephant in a china shop': the elephantine strength matters more for the fate of china than the elephant's intentions – that is, if it has a specific intention and follows it consistently.

Alternatively, we could repeat after Arnold Toynbee (in his broadcast of 14 July 1954): 'America is a large, friendly dog in a very small room. Every time it wags its tail it knocks over a chair.'

The strength of the American superpower is indeed breathtaking and mind-boggling: the US federal budget for 2003 takes US military expenditure to 40 per cent of the sum total of money spent on arms in the world. 'It exceeds the spending of the next 24 states combined, and is 25 times greater that the combined spending of all seven "rogue states" identified by the US as its enemies.'[6] Such a massive accumulation of weapons, not even remotely approximated, let alone matched, by anyone else, puts America in a militarily unassailable position. In consequence, as Michael Ignatieff points out, America is 'the only nation that polices the world through five global military commands; maintains more than a million men and women at arms on four continents, deploys carrier battle groups on watch in every ocean, guarantees the survival of countries from Israel to South Korea'.[7]

Coercive force is the sole resource which the US can resort to at any time without undue delay and of which it can be sure: weapons under its command are without doubt unequalled and inimitable by anybody on the planet. The capacity of weapons (what the weapons can be used for and what kind of job they are good – meaning unquestionably superior – at doing) determines their possible uses; and so the natural first reaction to crisis (in its original, Hippocratic meaning of a moment calling for decision and action) is war. And as Montesquieu famously concluded from his insight into the story of the Roman Empire, an empire founded by war has to maintain itself by wars.

An empire can choose the wars it intends to wage (though it may not choose to abstain from choosing a war to be waged), but the choices tend to be determined by the weapons in its possession. That is what Tzvetan Todorov found in the recent American decision to launch a war against Iraq in spite of what must have been obvious to everyone involved – that bombing and invading Iraq would not bring closer the war's manifest goal of annihilating terrorism, obviously a supranational and extraterritorial phenomenon. 'War against terrorism is not a simple task – it demands patience and tenacity. The war against Iraq was easy by comparison, it was sufficient to bomb the country to pulp under the pressure of an infinitely superior power.'[8]

Todorov points out that the latent yet hopefully rational cause of the Iraq war is difficult, perhaps even impossible, to locate. In cases when they do not bear testimony to inept reasoning, paucity of imagination or gross miscalculations and misjudgements among the planners, the publicly stated explanations are evidently duplicitous and dictated mostly by PR considerations: Saddam Hussein and Osama Bin Laden were each other's sworn enemies, not collaborators, and weapons of mass destruction were not in Iraq's possession. Even the explanation current among anti-war campaigners (that the wish to get hold of the second largest supply of crude oil in the world was the true reason for selecting Iraq as the target of war) gives little credit to the rationality of the war-planners: 'The war itself costs too much, the occupation the war provokes is ruinous, and all the benefits derived from the price of petrol are wiped out in advance by military expenditure.'[9]

All the same, the supposition that the recent focusing of US military might on the Middle East (Afghanistan, Iraq, possibly Iran, Syria and Saudi Arabia, not to mention the surreptitiously yet energetically expanding American military presence in the former Soviet republics of Asia) is, as David Harvey succinctly put it, 'all about oil'[10] is not to be

easily dismissed. As Harvey points out, 'the rate of exploitation of oil reserves has exceeded the rate of discovery since
1980 or so. Oil is slowly becoming increasingly scarce.'
Most of the extant supplies of crude oil are likely to be
completely depleted in a matter of ten to twenty years;
only the Middle Eastern oilfields promise to last another
half a century. Whoever controls the last remaining sources
of petrol on an increasingly petrol-thirsty and petrol-de-
pendent planet may hope to become a veritable kingmaker
of world politics and the bank-holder in the game of the
global economy – for as far into the future as the imagination of the managers of the capital stock reaches. 'What
better way for the United States to ward off the competition
and secure its own hegemonic position than to control the
price, conditions, and distribution of the key economic
resource upon which those competitors rely?' This is
indeed but a rhetorical question.

All the same, we may still argue that the very attempt to
seek and articulate a rational explanation of the war leads
away from the truth already revealed by Montesquieu.
There is no rational cause for war, and war does not
need rational causes. Being able to conduct a war at will
sums up all the rationality the empire's survival needs (or
rather can afford). The empire founds its hegemony on the
superior, ever-rising and technically perfected stocks of
sophisticated weapons which can be used only in the way
they were used in Iraq. And one rational element in the
string of reasonings that ended in the launching of smart
missiles against Iraq could be the realization that to sustain
its imperial position the empire must time and again put its
weapons on public and spectacular, and so convincing,
display.

Such displays would be likely to be regularly repeated
were the 'really existing' empire's power indeed as unpre-
cedentedly enormous as Brzezinski, Kissinger and their

soul-mates aver that it is: so infinite as to make light of
the limitations that troubled, and ultimately finished
off, the empires of the past. This, though, does not seem
to be the case. The present-day American variety of
empire can hardly equal the combined powers of the imperial centres of the colonial age – and it is the combined
power of imperial domination that carries weight in the
last account. The essential, though not the only weakness
of the American empire derives from its formation in the
closing years of that age, or perhaps even posthumously,
after its demise.

Empires governed by Europe may have varied – from the
prostrated giants on which the sun never set, all the way to
tiny and rather insignificant overseas enclaves, military
bases and trading posts. Because there were several really
existing empires and an indefinite and varying number of
would-be empires, the European states that ruled over
them may have acted as if they partook of a zero-sum
game, convinced that any advance of one particular colonial empire must lead inevitably not only to territorial
emaciation, but also to the fundamental weakening of
another. This was, however, a rather myopic and narrow-
minded view, sharply distinct from the image construed at
the receiving side of European colonial expansion. From
the perspective of those at the receiving side, the colonial
gains of any one European country *added* to the summary
strength of the colonialist enterprise. Just as the European
perspective collapsed the many-coloured variety of non-
European forms of life into one sorely truncated and flat-
tened image of 'the Orient', the variegated experience of
non-European peoples exposed to many and different colonial regimes and strategies pursued by European colon-
izers tended to mix, blend and condense into one
homogeneous notion of 'the West'. In the eyes of the

countries already invaded or living in fear of impending invasion, territorial conquests made by any one of the Europe-centred large and small empires enhanced the belief in 'the West's' incontestable superiority and invincibility. It indirectly reinforced the credibility of the belief in a unified and coordinated force deployed on the other side of the confrontation line; a belief that would puzzle and bewilder the Europeans locked in passionate and often gory conflicts with each other and engaged in recurrent wars – internecine, civil wars even if they were fought on the worldwide stage. In the eyes of the 'rest of the world' the cluster of European macro- and mini-empires blended into one worldwide and almighty Empire of the 'white man' – in no way inferior to, if not transcending, the might of the present-day American superpower.

Brzezinski's, Kissinger's, and similar declarations of the unprecedented volume and strength of US domination over the rest of the world derive their rationale from the absence of other empires and political/military units aspiring to, and capable of, empire-building efforts; of competitors hunting the same game and chasing the same trophies. Indeed, America is, and is likely to remain for a long time to come, alone in the field – the *sole* elephant in the planetary china shop. There are no other – able and willing, not to mention viable – candidates for the world-imperial role. This does not mean, though, that the powers of the new empire are necessarily less constrained than the combined powers of Western imperialism of yore – let alone that it enjoys the unlimited freedom to act that stubbornly evaded the West in the heyday of imperialist colonization. The opposite may well be the case, or yet transpire to be the case, given the profound changes that have taken place in the state of the world and in the chances of effective intervention in its affairs since the peak years of the 'old imperialism'.

To start with, the United States's bid for planetary hegemony comes after all the empires previously established have, one by one, been successfully fought back against, dismantled, forced to retreat or pressured to implode. That accumulated experience of protracted and in the end effective anti-colonialist resistance has sapped the myth that was collectively built and galvanized, the myth of the invincibility of the West and 'the White Man'. 'The West', of which the US army is now not just the most powerful but perhaps the only military arm and constantly flexed muscle, no longer looks indomitable. Its vulnerability is common knowledge, its continuous superiority is anything but a foregone conclusion, and resistance no longer looks hopeless.

The era of territorial expansion, invasion, annexation of invaded lands and their colonization is by and large over, notwithstanding a few sporadic hiccups of memory or ill-calculated or thoughtless 'gut reactions'. Power is no longer measured by the size of the territory administered; occupied lands have turned from an asset into a liability, an awkward burden better to be avoided. In our present era of post-space (or 'speed-space', to use Paul Virilio's term), the conquest of foreign lands and territorial acquisitions more generally are no longer the stakes of war; 'the last on the battlefield' is seldom the winner. The chores and the costs of cleaning up the mess and removing or defusing the toxic debris left by military action are gladly 'subsidiarized' to the vanquished; indeed, being assigned that unwholesome, unenviable task is the ultimate proof of defeat.

Territorial occupation, if undertaken, is viewed by all sides as a temporary event. For the winners, it is more an unpleasant necessity than a matter of deliberate and prudent choice: a temporary nuisance, an anomaly and an emergency measure to last only until 'normality' is restored and the alert can be called off. The preferred strategy of armed conflict is 'hit and run': putting the appointed enemy out of action and so opening up the resources it commanded to the uses dictated by the victor, while avoiding any long-term engagement in the daily running of the affairs of the devastated land and its disempowered population. If the word 'empire' is to be deployed at all under such radically transformed circumstances, marked by fundamental changes in the nature of the power game and its stakes and strategy, it should only be used, as Jacques Derrida advised, in the knowledge that it is *sous rature* – in full consciousness of its departure from its conventional meaning.

'Should be', however, does not mean that it will. The odds are against. Using terms *sous rature* (a common habit deeply rooted in vernacular practice) is a notorious source of semantic confusion: infesting the referents with lingering 'ghost meanings' that cloud instead of clarify their understanding and all too often prompt and motivate patterns of response that once were tried and tested but are presently out-of-date and inadequate. Perhaps the most striking examples of responses that have gone astray are the ones supplied by the metropolis of the 'ghost empire' (an updated version of the similarly ghostly 'Holy Roman Empire', grossly at odds with the realities of the Middle Ages): impromptu, improvised campaigns devised ad hoc with little if any consultation, on the assumption that, in the absence of other agents able and/or eager to compete for ecumenical hegemony, America 'can do it alone', disregarding opinions not backed by arsenals – just as it can, with impunity, ignore the arsenals themselves, so evidently inferior to its own. Such campaigns more often than not misfire. Sooner or later, reality emerges from behind the shattered illusion and the lesson is learned (the hard way) – though the lesson is usually memorized for only so long as it takes to replenish the arsenals and push the arms differential yet a few notches further. Frustration invariably calms down the warlike animus the moment the war is 'won' (though the criteria of victory are vexingly vague at a time when wars are a continuation not so much of politics as of its absence, and are waged mostly because one can get away, unpunished, with waging them), and when the time comes to make good the material damage and social havoc left in the wake of military action. Empire proceeds/plods/stumbles from one war episode to another by fits and starts, and its daily existence is punctuated by as many retreats as advances, though by few if any periods of calm and retrenchment.

The new 'empire' cannot stand still. It is more like the wind than a rock; it would disappear the moment it stopped blowing. It is the movement that counts, not the final destination or the momentarily pursued direction. Just as the ghosts exist solely in the modality of haunting ('ghosts' are 'sense-making' interpretations of a house being haunted), the new 'empire' persists on the condition of constantly reminding the world of its imperial presence. The new 'empire' is not an entity that could be drawn on a map (unless that map is simply an aerial snapshot of currently ongoing imperial campaigns and their momentary traces), but a way of being. Troops come and go, and it is not so much their staying power that keeps the spectre of empire hovering over the planet as their irresistible ability to arrive uninvited at the time of their choice and to leave with little warning as quickly as the generals wish.

Troops do not parachute in to spearhead a new order and new rules of human coexistence. 'Regime change', 'toppling a dictator', 'paving the way to democracy' or 'setting people free' soon prove to be not much more than PR slogans, however firmly (or sincerely) those who

deployed them to justify the war might have believed in
their truth. As John Pilger found when he explored the
state of affairs in one of the theatres of such wars, 'two
years ago, as the bombs began to drop, George Bush
promised Afghanistan "the generosity of America and its
allies". Now familiar old warlords are regaining power,
religious fundamentalism is renewing its grip and military
skirmishes continue routinely.'[11] Everything has fallen
from the frying pan into the fire. A report by Human
Rights Watch documents 'army and police troops con-
trolled by the warlords kidnapping villagers with impunity
and holding them for ransom in unofficial prisons; the
widespread rape of women, girls and boys: routine extor-
tion, robbery and arbitrary murder'. All that done 'by
gunmen and warlords who were propelled into power by
the United States and its coalition partners after the Tali-
ban fell in 2001'. Since October 2001 more than 10 billion
dollars has been spent on Afghanistan, ostensibly on its
'reconstruction'; 80 per cent of that generous sum has
been spent however on bombing the country and paying
the warlords. Pilger quotes a state department official who,
in a private briefing held as early as January 1997, ex-
pressed the hope that Afghanistan would become 'an oil
protectorate, like Saudi Arabia'. When it was pointed out
to him that Saudi Arabia had no democracy and perse-
cuted women, he retorted: 'We can live with that.'

Drawing a map of the empire would also be a pointless
exercise because the most conspicuously 'imperial' trait of
the new empire's mode of being consists in viewing and
treating the whole of the planet, simultaneously or intermittently, as a potential grazing ground and/or the con-
tainer of explicit or hidden, present or future threats to the
well-being of the metropolits. The 'topical relevancies'
that cast certain segments of the globe into the limelight
while rendering and keeping other segments invisible shift

depending on the current and itself eminently shifty defin-
itions of metropolitan interests.

By contrast to the imperial metropolises of yore, the US
is no longer interested in territorial acquisitions and actively desists from managerial/administrative engagements
outside its borders. As Benjamin R. Barber puts it, America 'blinks and turns inward, gazing overseas only to fix its
baleful eye on "enemy" targets defined by an elusive war
on terrorism and quixotically selected "rogue states"
meant to stand in for terrorists too difficult to locate and
destroy'.[12] As seen from the metropolis, the locations and
borders of the American *hinterland* or *Lebensraum* areas
follow shifts in the perception of metropolitan interests
and of threats to metropolitan security. As the borders
shift, so do the circumferences of friendly, hostile and
indifferent segments of the planet – of 'allied', 'enemy'
and client states. The empire's mode of being undermines
the value and significance of borders, while the scattered
punitive escapades of the imperial army sap ever anew the
assumption of every and any state's territorial sovereignty.

Curiously, it is not just the territorial sovereignty of
other states that is undermined. The metropolis becomes
a 'collateral casualty' of the process, and this is another
feature that sets it apart from the metropolises of yore. On
the one hand, it is an incapacity to 'balance the books' in
the framework of one state, however large, rich and powerful, that prompts the American metropolis to seek global
solutions to internal, but internally insoluble, problems
(like the supply of cheap energy or limits on the redundancy of labour and its potentially devastating social/polit-
ical repercussions) and to engage in the course of that
search in 'imperialist' actions. On the other hand, while
the actions may be politically motivated, they can hardly
be politically guided. The range of political options is fairly
limited, and as a rule the government must share the

target-choosing procedure with – and all too often surrender it to – potent economic powerhouses it does not control.

'Nation-states increasingly lose both their capacities for action and the stability of their collective identities,' as Jürgen Habermas observes. 'There is a crippling sense that national politics have dwindled to the more or less intelligent management of a process of forced adaptation to the pressure to shore up purely local positional advantages.'[13] Governments are reduced to the tactics of *Standortkonkurrenz* ('locational competition') to seduce freefloating global capital to flow in and to cajole it to resist the temptation to flow out.

If you are looking for a vivid demonstration of the pedlar/beggar role to which governments have been reduced in their struggle to keep their subjects alive and away from mischief, you need look no further than the website of the British Department of Trade and Industry – run by 'New Labour' – which, as Polly Toynbee recently observed, 'sells Britain as a low-wage, low-labour-protection nation'.[14] You would find there that 'total wage costs in the UK are among the lowest in Europe', that in the UK 'employees are used to working hard for their employers [sic!]', that 'in 2001 the average of hours worked a week was [in Britain] 45.1 for males and 40.7 for females', whereas 'the EU average was 40.9 per week', that 'UK law does not oblige employers to provide a written employment contract', and that the UK 'has the lowest corporation tax rate of any major industrialized country'.

It is not just governments handicapped by presiding over lesser and economically weaker states whose hands are tied. In the absence of a truly supranational network of political and juridical institutions capable of 'normatively regulating' the capricious and often haphazard drifts of already supranational capital, even the government of the world's sole superpower, proclaimed as the metropolis of a planet-wide empire, finds itself in much the same plight. As Richard Rorty pointed out as long ago as 1996.

> the central fact of globalization is that the economic situation of the citizens of a nation state has passed beyond the control of the laws of that state. It used to be the case that a nation's laws could control, to an important and socially useful extent, the movement of that nation's money. But now that the financing of business enterprise is a matter of drawing upon a global pool of capital, so that enterprises in Belo Horizonte or in Chicago are financed by money held in the Cayman Islands by Serbian warlords, Hong Kong gangsters and the kleptocrat presidents of African republics, there is no way in which the laws of Brazil or the US can dictate that money earned in the country will be spent in the country, or money saved in the country invested in the country.[15]

As to the 1 per cent of Americans who own 40 per cent of the country's wealth, Rorty explains elsewhere, 'their dividends typically increase when jobs are exported from Ohio to South China, and from North Carolina to Thailand.'[16] Little wonder that 'they have less and less at stake in America's future.' The idea that what is good for General Motors (or Microsoft for that matter) is good for America no longer sounds self-evident or even credible, if it ever did. Following Michael Lind and Edward Luttwak, Rorty prognosticates a time when one-fifth of the US population, its well-educated 'professional' part, will 'carry out the orders of the international super-rich'. Their loyalties may well lie elsewhere than those of the remaining four-fifths of the nation. The democratic deficit, widening steadily in all the countries engaged in 'locational competition' and hoping against hope to 'square the circle' (to save whatever remains of their legitimacy to rule at a time when their own capacity to influence, let alone determine, their citizens' living conditions is weakening by the day), affects the metropolis of the planetary empire no less, if no more, than it does the furthest or the most disempowered periphery on the globe.

Mike Mormile joined the LTV steel plant in Cleveland, Ohio, at the age of twenty-one. Thirty-two years later, on 19 December 2002, the day when LTV became insolvent and called in the receivers, he was made redundant, together with 56,000 other employees of the company (in all, 250,000 American steel workers have lost their jobs in recent years).[17] Mike Mormile lost 65 per cent of his pension fund and he lost, overnight, his and his family's medical insurance. The two remaining steel corporations, ISC and US Steel, purchased a small number of the bankrupt plants at a derisory price, cut in half the labour time allowed to produce a ton of steel, but refused to assume responsibility for the rights and entitlements earned by their employees through their past working lives. Just a few of former steelmen were offered employment in the much emaciated, asset-stripped plants. The total output of the salvaged steel plants is now considerably below the level of American demand: the gap is filled with steel imported from countries where workers are paid much less than in the US and where trade union protection is either non-existent or even less effective than in today's United States. Leo Gerard, the president of the United Steelworkers of America, opines that 'the United States has become the outlet for the surplus product of the global steel industry.'

Steel is but one of many products, and the US 'national economy' (another term that derives its present meaning mostly from an actuarial fiction sustained by a bookkeeping convention rather than a real 'totality', and one that for this reason ought only to be used, if at all, *sous rature*) is but one of many 'national economies'. The point is, though, that even the country deemed to be, claiming to be, and/or viewed as the metropolis of the worldwide empire is anything but shored up against the adverse impact of those deregulated and to a large extent extraterritorial, unanchored and free-floating economic forces now able to effectively defy all and any locally imposed constraints. Just as other governments are, the federal administration of the United States is left with virtually no option but to engage in *Standortkonkurrenz*. Just as in other countries, its attempts to lure volatile capital to the home pitch and keep it at home cannot but be lukewarm and half-hearted; no wonder they meet with only mixed success.

This said, there are reasons to suspect that the plight of the American economy is still worse than can be judged from reading the increasingly worrying statistics of 'economic growth', and particularly of the distribution of 'national wealth'. The national debt of the US is exorbitant. America lives on credit provided by (or extorted from) the rest of the world; it nevertheless spends prodigiously, and spends a lot of money it did not earn. David Harvey calculates that foreigners now own a third of the government debt and 18 per cent of the corporate debt of the US. The US 'now depends on over 2 billion dollars a day of net foreign investments inflow to cover its continuously rising current account deficit with the rest of the world'.[18] This, Harvey concludes, 'renders the US economy extraordinarily vulnerable to capital flight'. The question of whether such a situation, unthinkable in the case of lesser, 'ordinary' national economies, can be sustained in the long run, and how long that run may continue, is an ominous and potentially cataclysmic variable in the imperial equation. It is also everybody's guess . . .

In his trenchant book-long condemnation of the American-led worldwide empire, Benjamin Barber argues that the current conduct of American leaders (endorsed and supported by the opinion of the 'average American') is a logical sequel to the American isolationism of a century ago.

There is indeed a clear element of continuity between the two apparently opposite stances: a sort of a 'meta-assumption' that shows them to be but two varieties of the same worldview. According to that assumption, America is doomed to rely on *its own* guts and wits, America's destiny is to do whatever is to be done *alone*. Hence the commandment: America should keep others at a distance, accept their help when help is for the taking but remember that once the moment of truth and reckoning arrives it will be up to the Americans and only them to save the day. America should beware false, shifty and unreliable friends (and most friends are such) as much as, or even more than, it should beware explicit enemies – since there is no telling how long the friendship of even the most sincere of friends will be on offer. Practical precepts are drawn from that commandment in the American philosophy of life, addressed to all levels of human interaction – from the subtitle 'Trust no one' of the hugely popular 'real TV' show, *Survivor*, to Rumsfeld's insistence that any coalitions the US may put together for the purpose of the next military operations must be 'ad hoc' and stay 'flexible', and George Bush's verdict that 'who is not with us, is against us'.

American unilateralism chimes well with the experience of American history recast into truths deemed unquestionable for the simple reason of never having been submitted to questioning. It also chimes well with the good sense of the 'average American', immune to doubts since inoculated against the temptation of questioning. 'The course of this nation', insists George W. Bush, 'does not depend on the decisions of others'[19] – and one could be excused for thinking that it was an earlier President, Monroe, not the self-proclaimed world leader, speaking. Barber observes that *both* camps among the American political elite (which he brands respectively 'Eagles' and 'Owls', both hunters, but the first rash, impetuous and reckless, the second circumspect, calculating and cunctatory) 'are fixed on the sovereign right of an independent United States and of its "chosen people" to defend itself where, when, and how it chooses against enemies it alone has the right to identify and define'.[20] Indeed, the sole difference between the past isolationist and the present-day unilateralist stance is the radical expansion of the space inside which American interests need to be defended and where America remains, in the ultimate account, their solitary protector – the only power able and wishing to make American interests safe and keep them safe.

On 29 June 2003, Paul Bremer, the US administrator in occupied Iraq, left little to the imagination and even less to bargaining or negotiation: 'We dominate the scene and we will . . . impose our will on this country'[21] – the tacit, or not so tacit assumption being that the 'we' who impose their will are those who dominate the scene and that 'dominating the scene' is sufficient ground for the will's imposition. The statement showed a lot of self-confidence but little foresight. At the time it was made, Iraq in Mark Seddon's words was 'smouldering into guerrilla warfare', while Baghdad remained a 'looted, threatening place where the new "provisional coalition authority" can't even get the lights to work'. Since then, lights in the headquarters buildings may have been switched on, but they have failed to illuminate Iraq's future. Guerrilla warfare has anything but calmed down, with the ranks of those who wage it swelling together with the number of its direct and collateral victims. To what extent, if at all, the occupying troops 'dominate the scene' has become a question growing mooter by the day.

But how relevant to the present-day worries of the hapless emperor is the 'domination of the scene'?

Jacques Derrida articulates the problem that has by now turned into a truism: on our globalized planet terrorists do not wage a 'war', and the idea of a 'war against terrorism' is either a distant and misleading allegory or a meaningless concept.[22] Contemporary global (and globally conceived, born and groomed) terrorism does not match any of the three kinds of war which Carl Schmitt, a mere half-century ago, could view matter-of-factly as providing an exhaustive classification of wars: an interstate war, a civil war and a partisan (guerrilla) war. In terrorist activity, the link between violence and territory has been all but broken.

Jürgen Habermas moves a step further. Having admitted that the term 'war' could be used by the American leaders because it is less vulnerable to contestation than its alternatives, he considers the adoption of the term a gross error from the 'normative' as well as 'pragmatic' point of view. The use of the term 'war' is an error from the normative point of view because it elevates criminals to the rank of enemy soldiers, but it is also an error from the pragmatic point of view because 'it is impossible to wage a war (since this is what one must do to preserve the meaning of the term however it is defined) against a "network" which one is at pains to identify.'[23]

We may add: responding to terrorism by 'waging a war', at least in the form in which the collection of acts summarily called 'the war' have so far been undertaken, is not a 'continuation of politics' by those who declare and conduct the war. The point is, after all (to quote Barber again), that terror succeeds in what it promises rather than in what it actually achieves, and so turns the effort to defend against it into its chief tool . . . The terrorist can sit in a mountain cave or Karachi slum and watch his enemies self-destruct around the initial fear he has seeded with a single and singular act of terror or with a few well-chosen follow-up threats . . . [24]

By common opinion, the supreme objective of the terrorists is to paralyse and incapacitate an enemy whom they are much too weak to confront in open battle – by prodding and manoeuvring that enemy into a permanent state of insecurity and fear. The weapons the terrorists possess or those they can procure would look laughably primitive if they were displayed at an arms-trade fair alongside the hottest technology and state-of-the-art gadgets brought out of the warehouses and R&D laboratories of the military superpower. The terrorists, though, enjoy one enormous advantage over the most powerful arms and their users: they can enlist the superpower's resources – its numerous public address systems and ubiquitous security devices unequalled when it comes to the sowing and cultivation of a 'besieged fortress' mentality – to help their own strategy of sowing fear and to secure its success.

And the terrorists, unlike the large battalions and their heavy weapons, can move swiftly, surreptitiously and with no warning. In this art they have no equals – and so it is the turn of the superpower to dream, in vain, of matching the other's agility. Faithful replicas of the new globetrotting elite and the extraterritorial capital represented by that elite, terrorists need no clumsy, bulky and awkward supply columns that might curb their freedom of movement. They will not be stopped by the military waging territorial wars, just as global finances will not be arrested or so much as slowed down by politicians desperately trying to ground their power to act in territorially defined sovereignty. Attempts to pinpoint the terrorist army as if it consisted of columns marching to and fro between fortified military bases are both misbegotten and lamentably ineffective.

Willy-nilly, imperial powers must try to match the 'terrorist mode', though the means available to the terrorists are barred to them. For that reason, they cannot afford to stop trying, however futile – since inconclusive – their attempts are bound to prove. They feel obliged to top past investments with ever new ones and literally 'throw good money after bad'. In Barber's words, the US 'must repeatedly extend the compass of its power to preserve what it already has, and so is almost by definition always overextended'.[25]

However dramatic, spectacular and eminently 'photo-opportune' they are, the sporadic and scattered terrorist acts, even if multiplied in the public consciousness by the much more numerous, repetitive and increasingly regular intelligence warnings of more to come, present only one symptom of the global 'frontier-land' in which everything may happen and nothing can be done once and for all, where rules are made only to be breached, where 'hit and run' tactics are the sole effective mode of acting, and where those who master such arts rule supreme (until they are outsmarted by their keen and intelligent understudies, that is). In that 'frontier-land' laid out by the massive deregulation and emancipation of the capitalist economy from past local (read: nation-state's) constraints, expanded reproduction and violent dispossession (as Harvey puts it[26]) proceed hand in hand and are seldom, if ever, distinguishable from each other.

In Harvey's terminology, global capital reproduces itself, as well as the conditions of its own continuous self-reproduction, by deploying as its major weapon 'accumulation by dispossession': that is, 'the periodic creation of a stock of devalued, and in many instances undervalued, assets in some part of the world, which can be put to profitable use by the capital surpluses that lack opportunities elsewhere'.[27] At the time of the Asian financial crisis of 1997–8, for instance, the combination of 'massive devaluation, IMF-pushed financial liberalization, and IMF-facilitated recovery' led, as R. Wade and F. Veneroso have argued, to 'the biggest peacetime transfer of assets from domestic to foreign owners in the past fifty years in the world'.[28]

Capital and the military follow strikingly similar 'hit-and-run' tactics. Heretofore 'virgin' (from the marketing point of view) lands, or types of goods that have never before been included in market circulation and assigned an exchange value (state-provided services and state-administered public properties, previously non-commodified resources like water, genetic stock, intellectual products, or even historical tradition and memories), are now targeted for 'commodification'. Their assets are stripped, the stock-holders' profits are temporarily inflated, and after that capital moves swiftly to other meadows not yet used up by protracted grazing, leaving behind the masses of the expropriated – the 'human waste' of the latest chapter in the story of capitalist development.

Whereas the substance of hit-and-run tactics in the case of military escapades is the escape from responsibility for the damage perpetrated in the course of the military action and its consequences, in the case of capital the principle is to avoid responsibility for the consequences of dispossession – for the countless lives deprived of the means of survival and self-reproduction and so unlikely to resist the exploitation of labour 'emancipated' on capital's terms. In both cases, the most lethal weapon of the attackers is freedom of movement and its speed: their capacity to fly away from the battlefield the moment all the spoils have been gathered, all the assets have been stripped, when any further destruction won't be 'creative', and to abandon the 'waste-disposal' task to the defeated and dispossessed 'locals'. The credible danger of capital flying away is the principal factor in rendering the 'liberated' human capital – now disabled and evicted from productive/livelihood-earning action – amenable to commodification and exploitation.

A 'frontier-land' has a strictly limited life expectation unless it expands extensively and intensively. In these hit-and-run tactics, the empire transforming the planet into a frontier-land seeks the magic formula of its own survival. There is reciprocal feedback between the frontier-land conditions and the capitalism of the globalization era.

The 'new empire' exists in the realm of a frontier-land. This is the only realm where it can breathe freely; the only space where it can monotonously resuscitate the conditions of its survival and replenish the sources of its vitality.

'It is time to stop pretending that Europeans and Americans share a common view of the world, or even that they occupy the same world' – this is, let us recall, the verdict of Robert Kagan, a member of the Carnegie Endowment for International Peace. Europeans, he says, 'believe they are moving beyond power into a self-contained world of laws and rules and transnational negotiation and cooperation' – whereas the United States 'remains mired in history, exercising power in the anarchic Hobbesian world where international rules are unreliable and where security and promotion of a liberal order still depend on the possession and use of military might'.[29]

Suddenly Europe has found itself in an unfamiliar – unprecedented, unexplored, unmapped – position. After centuries of immersing itself with relish in the Hobbesian *bellum omnium contra omnes*, particularly (though by no means solely) outside its borders, it has now mellowed into an acceptance of the Kantian model of perpetual peace. The irony is that it has arrived at this point inside a Hobbesian planet grounded in the rejection of that model, which it did quite a lot to help strike roots.

In the eyes and the practice of today's Europe, the maxim 'might is right' is no longer acceptable – but the sceptics would jibe that the maxim lost its credibility in European eyes because it stopped being a weapon in European hands. Weakened and relegated to a secondary and dependent status, Europe cannot strive for what it believes is right while relying on its present, grossly inadequate might. Behind Kagan's argument lurks a belief that the reality of a Hobbesian world is a welcome bonus, and the first preference, for those who can afford it, for the powerful and vigorous, whereas the dream of a Kantian perpetual peace is a consolation for the weak or an apology for the failed and jaded: just the kind of opinion one would expect to be conceived, promoted, and daily corroborated in a frontier-land.

One should write to Kagan's credit that he hardly tries to conceal that opinion, even if he stops short of articulating it explicitly. All the same, he goes so far as to point out that Europe can indulge in its dreams only courtesy of the US, which has taken it upon itself to make the Hobbesian world amenable to human habitation. 'Europe's Kantian order depends on the United States using power according to the old Hobbesian rules.'

Étienne Balibar offers a highly illuminating comment on Kagan's portrayal of the present plight of Europe, painted with the palette of American imperial interests:

> I don't believe I distort the meaning of Kagan's analysis if I say in a nutshell: the 'European' position, expressing

something like a religion of law, is at the same time *power-less* ('how many divisions, Europe?' we might ask, echoing Stalin) and *illegitimate* (since it disguises a historical regression as moral progress, misrepresenting its real weakness as an imaginary strength). Finally, it is *self-destructive*, since it undermines the defense capacities of the western democracies . . . It is decidedly not America that has 'too much power', but Europe that has too little . . . [30]

One is tempted to wonder, though, whether US militancy coupled with the enormity of American power, and Europe's lack of comparable military strength combined with the peace-loving sentiments of the Europeans – each a calamity in each other's eyes – do not make a truly explosive mixture when they meet on the same planet at the same historical time. This compound is indeed inherently unstable, threatening a catastrophe of incalculable proportions. It is a sorry moment for humanity when the ability to act reflectively and the willingness to act ethically retreat to different camps.

Especially here and now, when the interest in survival and 'moral progress' need each other as never before. Neither can be satisfied without the other. Both dictate the same imperatives for action and the same strategy. As a secure existence can no longer be guaranteed to lands and populations singly or severally (under conditions of planetary interdependence, security of any part of the globe can be achieved only inside a secure humanity), ethically illuminated global action, aimed at defending humans everywhere against indignity and mitigating the growing inequality of human chances and the rising volume of social injustice and human humiliation, is the most fundamental condition of shared survival in any one of the many senses of that notion.

Another aspect of the present planetary condition has become increasingly clear (or rather, for those aware of history, emphatically reconfirmed) over recent years: left alone, the 'Hobbesian world' is utterly unlikely to 'reform itself'. Its pernicious and in the end ruinous impact on all parts of the globe and their interaction is, on the contrary, most likely to exacerbate itself and reveal its inherent tendency to run out of control. No one can feel safe; no one, not even the winner of today, is exempt from that rule and sufficiently fortified against that danger. Gains that players may draw from the continuing free-for-all are endemically unsafe, and the costs of their defence grow by the day even if the price of human lives wasted in the name of their defence is left out of account.

Just when the ultimate victory of freedom (as embodied in the free market) has been announced, the global economy has entered its most turbulent and frightening decade. David Harvey's poignant and juicy description of that memorable time deserves to be quoted at length:

> During the 1990s there was no clear enemy and the booming economy within the United States should have guaranteed an unparalleled level of contentment and satisfaction throughout all but the most underprivileged and marginalized elements in civil society. Yet . . . the 1990s turned out to be one of the most unpleasant decades in US history. Competition was vicious, the avatars of the 'new economy' became millionaires overnight and flaunted their wealth, scams and fraudulent schemes proliferated, scandals (both real and imagined) were everywhere embraced with gusto . . . (Ir)rational exuberance prevailed over common sense, and corporate corruption of the political process was blatant. Civil society was, in short, far from civil. Society seemed to be fragmenting and flying apart at an alarming rate. It seemed . . . in the process of collapsing back into the aimless, senseless chaos of private interests.[31]

The war won, and especially the war won finally and irrevocably as Francis Fukuyama proclaimed, proved to be a more sinister and toxic danger than the hazards of an ongoing battle and of outcomes still in the balance. And so another war was prescribed as the patented remedy for the ailments of victory . . . Under the circumstances, as Harvey observes, 'the engagement with Iraq was far more than a mere diversion from difficulties at home; it was a grand opportunity to impose a new sense of social order at home and bring the commonwealth to heel.' At a price, of course, and an enormous and daily rising price, paid mostly by democracy and civil liberties. 'Criticism was silenced as unpatriotic. The evil enemy without became the prime force through which to exorcise or tame the devils lurking within.'

The 'Fukuyama world', if it ever comes into being, may be nothing else than another rendition of the Hobbesian world. The absence of a viable adversary incarnating a viable alternative is the true Achilles heel of a triumphant and rampant, free-floating and all-penetrating global capitalism. Its major, potentially terminal misfortune is the absence of effective resistance. On a Fukuyaman/Hobbesian planet, USA military might, the strong arm, trailblazer and police force of global capitalism can deliver blows at will and at random ('in the place of its choice, at the time of its choice'), fearing little and hoping to emerge from the short, sharp encounter undamaged; but it is precisely that hope that sustains and invigorates the Hobbesian world and makes of the nebulousness of its Kantian alternative a self-fulfilling prophecy.

For half a century, a formidable, fearsome and all-too-real enemy defended capitalism against the morbid consequences of its most wearisome and worrisome excesses. Capitalism would probably have conquered that enemy with little difficulty, had the confrontation been limited to a race run on capitalism's running track – as it did in the end, once the reproduction of that enemy's staunch and uncompromising alterity lost its inner impetus. As long as the enemy was not just another competitor in the same race, but a genuine 'other', a carrier of an alternative mode of life, it could induce capitalism to self-limit and self-correct. This is the kind of adversary that is now conspicuously missing. In its triumphant, seemingly unstoppable march through the planetary casino, capital confronts instead numerous competitors eager to play the same game and keen to throw their assets into the bank, or bank robbers uncertain of their chances at the table and so looking for a short-cut to the reversal of fortune. One variety of adversaries that capital does not come across are the proponents and realistic embodiments of an alternative form of life that would entail the abolition of the casino. In its conquest of the globe, the new global capitalism scores successive victories under the sign of the Absent Alternative. It is under that sign that it may perish.

May Europe fill that vacancy? Can Europe offer, can Europe be, the Alternative? There was a time when this seemed to be a realistic prospect.

Licking the wounds of the last local conflict played on the global stage, and squeezed between the nightmarish vision of the totalitarian *Gleichschaltung* advancing from the Near East and its own nightmarish memories of the devastating, and ultimately gory, domestic consequences of *Standortkonkurrenz*, Europe set out to work hard, for thirty glorious years, on the great social experiment of mitigating the unacceptable extremes of unbridled capitalism with 'socialism with a human face', while averting the unbearable consequences of the raw and uncouth communist version of social equity with 'capitalism with a

human face'. Europe was searching, so to speak, for a
'third way' *avant la lettre*.

The result was a *social state*. That is, a state offering to all
its citizens a collectively endorsed and financed insurance
policy against individual and categorial injuries unavoidable in a capitalist economy, and a state that measured the
quality of the whole society by the quality of life of its
weakest and most sorely injured citizens.

There were, of course, numerous factors in addition to
the twin fears mentioned above that paved the way to the
combination of piecemeal reforms into the design, building and maintenance of a 'social state' – and all such
factors have been amply researched and recorded.[32] One
can argue, however, that all these factors jointly would not
have sufficed had it not been for the 'double bind' situation of Europe, set on a dangerous voyage between the
devil and the deep blue sea. It was the commonly accepted
sense of imminent danger and of the indisputable need to
navigate the middle route between two equally perilous
and fearsome rocks that enabled those factors to link together, intertwine, cohere and precipitate the postwar all-
European consensus.

Given the almost universal consensus on the nature of
the problem, and widespread support for the chosen solution, there was no shortage of political forces, articulated
or amenable to articulation, prepared to mobilize behind
the great experiment that was meant to put paid to Europe's endemic inclination to civil wars – whether of the
interstate or the cross-national, interclass variety. The
pride of place among such political forces belonged,
though, to Christian Democracy – the spiritual greenhouse
and political base of Adenauer, de Gasperi and Schumann,
the three statesmen mainly responsible for laying the foundation of a 'social policy' instead of a 'power politics'
Europe. They were joined by Paul-Henri Spaak, a social

democrat. Were I pressed to quantify the relative weight of the contributions, I would consider the party-political composition of the 'Big Four' as a fair guide. In its tradition, if not in its current political idiom, the Christian Democratic vision was essentially transnational: Europe was a 'Holy Empire' well before it was sliced into national domains. One could say that Christian Democracy was a new, multilingual rendition of the Latin-speaking spirit of Christian Europe; as such, it had fewer inhibitions than other political camps (including the social democrats, who had been trained since the start of the twentieth century and its forty years of hot and cold war to support their respective nationalisms, including the most chauvinistic and jingoist among them), and even less revulsion towards the idea of a transnational unification of the continent. Such transnationality – symbolized by Catholic France and Italy holding hands with Protestant Germany and qualifying the sacrosanct principle of national sovereignty that in the post-Westphalian era came to replace, and undermine, Christian unity – could be cast as a continuation, after a nationalist interlude three centuries long, of the unfinished business of Counter-Reformation; a restoration of a tested status-quo-ante, pan-European ecumenism rather than a leap into the unknown.

In the building and sustenance of the social state social democracy was the leading partner, simultaneously the brains trust and the executive agency. Indeed, over thirty postwar years the development of 'welfare' institutions and provisions became the trademark of the social democratic parties in virtually every European country. In time, concern with 'social insurance' became a distinguishing feature of European states – and remained a seldom questioned feature until the dawn of the 'neoliberal revolution' in the 1970s. The essence of that later revolution was the release of wealth production and wealth distribution from the state supervision and management that was intended by the social state model. In other words, the substance of the neoliberal turn was the surrender of the part of the nation-state's territorial sovereignty that was crucial for the 'book balancing' function of that model, and so also for meeting the responsibilities on which the legitimation of the states power rested during those heady 'glorious thirty' years.

The 'social state' model entailed, as its essential element, a target of 'full employment' – a shorthand term for the reassertion of every citizen's importance, indeed indispensability, for the wealth and welfare of society as a whole. The aim of full employment went hand in hand with the postulated fullness of citizenship: alongside the 'consumer side', the right to partake of the benefits from the growing national wealth, went the right to participate in the creation of that wealth, and consequently in the running of public (considered as common and shared) affairs, and to have a part in determining the nature of public (considered as common and shared) interests. If the collective endorsement and provision of social insurance against individually suffered misfortune reflected the intention to socialize the risks endemic to the capitalist economy and market competition, full and active citizenship signalled the effort of universal inclusion, through the body politic, in a society evolving towards the ideal type of community.

With the benefit of hindsight one can interpret the social state as (hopefully) a solution to the problem posited by Europe's retreat from its overseas colonial possessions.

The progressive efficiency of the modern capitalist/ market economy has been from the start paid for by a growing volume of 'redundant humans' – people for whom the new and improved, smarter and slimmer ways of wealth production had no use. For several centuries, that 'human waste' of economic progress could be disposed of in the vast expanses which, due to Europe's military and technological superiority, could be treated, for all practical intents and purposes, as 'no man's', or at any rate 'deserted' and 'underpopulated', and 'fallow' or 'undercultivated' land. Locally generated problems of redundancy, potentially explosive, found their global solutions. Once unleashed on the native precapitalist population of the colonized lands, however, the capitalist 'new and improved' economic model gradually transformed the conquered territories from 'waste-disposal tips' into huge and fast-growing factories of redundant humans. No longer could the potentially combustible cinder-heaps of surplus population turned out daily by economic progress at home be thinned out and at least partly unloaded overseas. The waste could only be defused and detoxified if it was recycled at home. The excluded had to be readmitted. The useless had to be made useful again. The denied social allocations, repositioned. The refused human dignity, rehabilitated. Above all, everyone – the temporarily downtrodden and currently fortunate alike – had to be reassured, nay made certain, that this was exactly what would happen if the need arose. For all such needs, the social state was looked to as a solution.

Letting capital out of that complex ethical/social/political equation meant the death-knell of the social state. Whatever remains of its institutions now has to wage an uphill struggle against the pressure of globally produced problems. European social states have now been faced with the impossible task of providing locally designed, administered and protected solutions to problems produced globally and beyond the reach of local control. Nation-states have only the strategy of *Standortkonkurrenz* to resort to, and that kind of interstate competition sets demands that militate against the most fundamental principles of the inclusive social state. The flip side of the effort to salvage the inclusive/ protective functions it was once hoped would be performed by the social state is its ultimate hopelessness; there are no local solutions to global problems, and a social state cannot be built and sustained in one territorially sovereign state taken on its own; perhaps not even inside a 'fortress' incorporating, for the sake of strengthened defence, a combination of several such states. The globalization of capital and trade, the removal of capital's local restraints and obligations, and the resulting extraterritoriality of major economic forces have made a 'social state in one country' all but a contradiction in terms.

The abrupt surrender of state control over capital's undertakings did not happen without resistance. There was a time following the Reaganite/Thatcherite coup d'état when Europeans voted social democrats back into power in thirteen out of fifteen member states of the European Union. It proved to be a short-lived episode, though. All over the place, though with varying degrees of conviction and zeal, the parties once identified with the project of the social state presided, once in government, over its further dismantling. Instead of reasserting public control over public resources, they ceded more national assets to the free play of market forces and made more resources once excluded from commodification amenable to profit-making and capital accumulation. Some did it enthusiastically, proclaiming their role reversal as a 'new and improved' rendition of old-fashioned and outdated social democratic lore, some reluctantly and under pressure – but all vociferously (even if sometimes shamefacedly) insisted that the 'new way' was the only way, and by making a dogma of the 'there is no alternative' slogan helped to bury all realistic and imaginable options.

As Allyson Pollock found, the true extent of the commodification of services that were once public could hardly be learnt from the newspaper headlines. In the UK, the piecemeal yet thorough and relentless phasing out of collective insurance provisions and the breaching of the most fundamental assumptions of the 'social state' model proceed surreptitiously, without ever having been vented in full in a public debate, let alone subjected to a democratically endorsed strategic decision. For instance, 'over the past twenty years the NHS has almost totally withdrawn from the provision of long-term care.' 'The primary responsibility for the care of frail or sick older people and those with disabilities is largely left to 5.7 million carers, of whom 600,000 provide unpaid care for fifty hours or more a week.' 'In 2001, 91 per cent of nursing home beds and 75 per cent of residential care beds in England were operated on a for-profit basis.'[33]

Progressively impoverished social state provisions gradually turned from tokens of citizens' rights into tools of social exclusion and symptoms/indications of social stigma – and so they fast lost their allure, together with residues of their electoral support. But the most prominent victim of the slaughter of alternative options was social democracy itself – as a viable political force with its own constituency and a distinctive political programme. Social democracy shared the lot of the social state it showed itself to be as willing to consign to history as other contestants in the political ring. In the process, it lost the raison d'être that made it a major political force and sustained it as one throughout the last century.

Jürgen Habermas concludes his study of the 'postnational constellation' with the following observations:

> Within the national sphere, the only one that they can currently operate in – they [political parties] have to reach out toward a European arena of action. And this arena, in turn, has to be programmatically opened up

with the dual objective of creating a social Europe that can
throw its weight onto the cosmopolitan scale.[34]

One of these observations conveys a crucially important
message: being (becoming, being resurrected as) a larger
rendition of the social state, Europe stands a chance of
acquiring a large enough weight to be felt when (if) it is
thrown on the 'cosmopolitan' scales; presumably, for two
reasons at once. Its 'social' nature would lend Europe as a
whole the degree of cohesion that once made nation-states
such effective and consequential fighting units; whereas the
collective competence of Europeans in the design, building
and running of a social state now raised to the level of a
confederation of states would be Europe's significant, attractive and welcome dowry that might yet further magnify
its role in the 'cosmopolitan' arena. Though only obliquely
and in a somewhat perverted fashion, Europe's political
leaders admit that much when they insist that the putative
'asylum seekers' are in fact attracted to Europe mostly by
its generous and inclusive social provisions.

One wonders, though, how that feat could be accomplished, given the current parlous state and bad press of
the 'social state' inside Europe itself, and particularly the
non-availability of viable agencies indispensable both for
curing the present ailments of social states in Europe and
then for the 'opening up' of a convalescent 'social' Europe
on the planetary stage.

'Let me assert my firm belief that the only thing we have to
fear is fear itself,' declared Franklin Delano Roosevelt in
his Inaugural Address of 4 March 1933, the speech that
sketched the vision of the New Deal, the overture to an
American brand of the social state.

Indeed, the great promise of the social state, the promise
that was to inform and guide the next half-century of

history, was *freedom from fear*. Human beings are powerful enough to deal with what pains them, and to muzzle what makes them suffer – except the fear of pain and suffering, and except at the moments when that fear deepens so much that it makes them impotent to act.

In retrospect, the social state episode may be best interpreted as a long counter-offensive against the fear that descended on Americans as much as on Europeans during the 'Great Depression' which tore the veil off the frailty of the social foundations on which every human's well-being – even the well-being of the most fortunate humans – rested. The awakening was brutal, shocking and (at least for the generation that experienced it) unforgettable. A Herculean effort was needed to stifle the fear it aroused. The project of freedom from fear pursued through the social state was perhaps the boldest endeavour ever consciously undertaken by humanity, along with the resolve it gathered to see it through.

On the road towards the social state many battles against fear have been won. The war, however, was anything but finished, and ultimate victory is no more in sight today than it was at the time of Roosevelt's Inaugural Address. The weapons of war suggested by Roosevelt or Beveridge and put into service are now being decommissioned en masse as no longer fit for the new brave world of universal commodification and global market rule, but fear has not stopped haunting nights and poisoning days. Neither has it vanished from political speeches; if anything, it has grown in stature, been made into the public enemy number one and a prime target of governmental crusades. 'Freedom from fear' remains, as before, the foremost item on each government's list of declared priorities, and a promise to which every politician seriously considering a seat in the government must pay at least lip-service.

The days of the *social* state may be grinding to an end, but most certainly not the heyday of the *security* state.

But was not security also the principal raison d'être of the social state? Of course it was. So what has changed? The *meaning* of the idea of 'security' has changed, and particularly the officially recognized causes of its stubborn *elusiveness*. As Miguel de Cervantes foreknowingly noted half a millennium ago (in chapter 20 of the first part of *Don Quixote*), 'fear has many eyes and can see things underground.' Fears may see what eyes cannot. Also what eyes never would. Good tidings for the fear, though bad news for the fearing: fears are fed, and made to grow through the eyes – through what the eyes see and even more assuredly through what they cannot.

The security we fear for, about which we are told and encouraged and groomed to be fearful, while being promised by the powers-that-be that it will be granted, is no longer the kind of security Roosevelt or Beveridge had in mind. It is not the security of our place in society, of personal dignity, of honour of workmanship, self-respect, human understanding and humane treatment, but instead a security of the body and of personal belongings. It is not security from those who refuse us jobs or deny our humanity when we are in a job, from those who take away our self-respect, and humiliate and dishonour us – but a security against trespassers on our property and strangers at the doorway, prowlers and beggars in the streets, sexual offenders at home and outside, poisoners of wells and hijackers of planes. Fears might grow from the same roots as before – but once they have sprouted they may be, and are, transplanted into different beds. In their new location the implements forged by the social state are useless. Other tools are called for. What used to be the proper weapon to fight unemployment, destitution in old age, social exclusion and social degradation is out of tune with the fight against terrorists. For each fear, its own tranquillizer.

There is one more – perhaps the most consequential – trait that sets contemporary fears apart from those which Roosevelt or Beveridge set themselves to uproot. Those fears were calamities pure and simple, afflictions that could be put to no good use, the all-too-real sufferings and torments that stood between people and their chances of a decent human life. They were also difficult to be mistakenly located; as Ulrich Beck has pointed out, the causes of such pains as hunger, disease or lack of life prospects, misery or destitution are difficult, nay impossible to mistake, as 'in the experience of material need, actual affliction and subjective experience of suffering are indissolubly linked.'[35] Not so with what Beck calls 'risks', chances that calamities currently in the sights of governmental guns will strike. 'Risks' are invisible – one needs to be told of their existence to fear them, and their causes are hardly ever transparent. Beck points out that because of their invisibility the very existence of risks, and certainly their gravity and intensity, may be denied (as, for instance, in the case of greenhouse gases or the warming up of the planet). But the invisibility of the new risks also has another and much more seminal consequence. Hunger is as unlikely to be imagined as it is to be denied – but threats to safety can be imagined, and easily. To quote Beck once more:

> *Interpretative diversions* of stirred-up insecurities and fears are more easily possible than for hunger and poverty. What is happening here need not be overcome here, but can be deflected in one direction or another and can seek and find symbolic places, persons, and objects for overcoming its fear. In risks consciousness then, *displaced* thought and action, or *displaced* social conflicts are especially possible and in demand.

To put it in a nutshell: 'safety risks' may be covered up or denied; but they may also be *invented*. As for the reasons to be fearful for safety, they may be kept secret or argued away; but they may also be fantasized, exaggerated or blown up out of all proportion.

The formidable Russian philosopher Mikhail Bakhtin pointed out that all earthly powers tend to excavate lodes of discipline from their subjects with the help of '*official* fear': an artificial, custom-made replica of '*cosmic* fear' – that natural and original horror felt by mortal, vulnerable and impotent human beings when faced with an all-powerful and inscrutable Nature.[36] If Bakhtin was right (and there is much to say for his suggestion in our times), then the *production* of 'official fear' is the key to the powers' effectiveness. Cosmic fear may need no human mediators, but official fear, like all other cultural artifices, cannot do without them. Official fear can only be *contrived*. Earthly powers do not come to the rescue of humans already gripped by fear – though they try everything possible, and more, to convince their subjects that this is indeed the case. Earthly powers, much like offers in consumer markets, must create their own 'clientele', and so their own demand. 'Fear capital' must first be produced for the earthly power to ingratiate itself and earn its subjects' allegiance by being tough on what the subjects are afraid of. For its grip to hold, human objects must be *made*, and *kept*, vulnerable, insecure, and frightened.

Bakhtin's conclusions must have been made much easier by the empirical evidence at his disposal at the time and place of his writing. Stalin, then in charge of Bakhtin's homeland, repeatedly demonstrated his power to launch purges and witch-hunts – but also his ability to stop or suspend them as abruptly and inexplicably as they had been started. There was no telling in advance which human pursuits would be branded next as cases of witchcraft. Blows fell at random, and bringing charges, not to mention supplying material proof of the link with the variety of witchcraft currently being hunted, was a frowned-upon luxury (as duly noted by Soviet popular wit, in the story of a hare explaining why he, a hare, runs for shelter when he hears that camels are currently being culled: 'they'd kill you first, and then you try to prove that you were not a camel . . . '). When *everyone* is vulnerable and uncertain *at all times* what the next morning may bring, it is survival and safety, *not* a sudden catastrophe, that appears to be a superhuman feat requiring a lot of foresight, wisdom and powers of action – all of them beyond the comprehension, resources and skills of ordinary human beings. Under Stalin's rule, it was the *withholding* of the randomly distributed blow, *exempting* a person from Siberian camps or a firing squad, that appeared to be the proof of the supreme power's potency, wisdom, fatherly care, benevolence and grace. For the favours one receives, one should be grateful. And one was.

Human vulnerability and uncertainty is the foundation of all political power. In the Stalinist variety of totalitarian power, that is in the absence of market-produced precariousness of the human condition, such vulnerability and uncertainty had to be produced and reproduced by the police forces under the command of the political power. It might have been more than a sheer coincidence that random terror was unleashed on the Russians on a massive scale at the same time as the last residues of the free market in Russia were wrapped up.

In a modern society of the capitalist and market-run variety, vulnerability, uncertainty and insecurity of existence are assured by the exposure of life pursuits to the hazards and vagaries of market competition. When they require discipline and law observance from their subjects, political powers may rest the legitimacy of their demands on the promise to mitigate the extent of the prevailing vulnerability and uncertainty, to limit the harm and damage perpetrated by the free play of market forces, to shield the vulnerable against at least the most devastating of the painful blows they do or may suffer, and to insure the insecure against the risks which all free competition necessarily holds in store.

Such legitimation, let me repeat, found its ultimate expression in the practices of the 'social state': based on the assumption that the insurance of each citizen against the blows of individual fate is the task and the responsibility of the community of citizens as a whole. That formula of political power, however, is presently receding into the past. The social state's institutions are one by one being dismantled or phased out, while the constraints previously imposed on business activities and on the free play of market competition and its consequences are one by one being removed. The protective functions of the state are being tapered to serve only a small minority of unemployable and invalid people (and they are no longer preventative; they are set in motion only after the disaster has struck). Even that minority tends to be reclassified, however, from an issue of social care into an issue of law and order, as an incapacity to participate in the market game increasingly tends to be criminalized. The state washes its hands of the vulnerability and uncertainty arising from the logic (or illogicality) of the free market, now recast as a private problem, a matter for individuals to deal with and cope with, each one on their own, with the resources in their private possession.

The unprepossessing side-effect of this trend is the sapping of the foundations on which state power has rested through a large part of modern times. The widely noted growth of political apathy, the loss of political interest and commitment ('no more salvation by society,' as Peter

Drucker famously put it) and a massive retreat by the population from participation in institutionalized politics all testify to the crumbling of the established foundations of state power. The message most commonly heard from the appointed spokespersons of the 'great society' is the call to be 'more flexible'. These days, uncertainty is offered as the cure for insecurity . . .

Having rescinded or severely reduced its previous programmatic interference with market-produced insecurity, contemporary states must seek other, non-economic varieties of vulnerability and uncertainty on which to rest their legitimacy. They act as if they have chosen to move *from social states to security states*. They shift the anxiety beefed up by the progressive deregulation of essential living conditions, the privatization of risks and the withdrawal of communal insurance over to the issue of personal safety: to fears arising from threats to human bodies, possessions and habitats emanating from criminals, the 'underclass', 'asylum seekers' carrying diseases and keen to engage in street crime, and most recently from global terrorism or weapons of mass destruction ready to be used in the next forty-five minutes.

Unlike the insecurity born of the market, which is if anything all too visible to overlook, that alternative insecurity which the state hopes will salvage its redemptive claims must be artificially whipped up, or at least highly dramatized and insistently, repeatedly, monotonously hammered home if it is to inspire sufficient 'official fear' and at the same time dwarf and push down the league table the worries of *economically* generated insecurity about which the state administration can do nothing and/or wishes to do nothing. Unlike the market-generated threats to livelihood and welfare which are best portrayed in pastel shades, the extent of the dangers to personal safety must be painted in the loudest of colours, so that the *non*-materialization of threats can be applauded as an extraordinary event, a result of the vigilance, care, prowess and goodwill of the state organs.

When they were brutally denied their flight connections, shuffled to and fro around overcrowded airport halls, refused their rights to privacy and cast as guilty until they proved their innocence, the hapless victims of an 'imminent terrorist attack' applauded the security guards – loudly, whole-heartedly. Who else would try so hard to disperse their fears – these fears right now, or any others? Who else would make sure that they arrived safely and in one piece from here to there?

This kind of fear, complete with the mechanism of its production and its uses, is a product of the Hobbesian world. It is also the main factor of that world's continuous resuscitation.

And so the same question comes back: can Europe offer, can Europe be, an alternative to the Hobbesian world of the planetary frontier-land brought into being, serviced and perpetuated by the new empire?

There are a few distinctly European, perhaps even uniquely European phenomena, some old and some new, that would suggest the answer 'yes' – though the odds on the other side are daunting. Calculation of the relative strengths of the factors 'pro' and 'con' cannot be pre-empted through theoretical argument; in the last account it can only be decided through political choices and resolve.

To start with, the ghost of the social state is unlikely to be exorcised. It will go on haunting the dark cellars and airy attics as well as all connecting floors of the joint European home – and the fame it has managed to earn worldwide will go on jogging the memory of Europeans. The social state has been a greenhouse of peaceful conflict resolution; or, to slightly paraphrase Balibar's terms, a workshop in which the tools of assuaging and taming conflict through its 'institutionalization' have been forged. The building and servicing of the social state have been and remain a lesson in the art of 'combining the different resources for *institutionalizing conflicts*', that is 'providing antagonistic interests with formal "representation" within the state, instead of suppressing and criminalizing them'.[37] Instead of repression and exclusion, a sustained effort to 'enable' the victims of injustice through a more equitable provision of (to use Amartya Sen's term) 'capabilities'. That art, practised and polished in Europe for many years, can be drawn upon now, when it comes to taming and civilizing the global frontier land – even if it will take more, much more than merely enlarging the tools successfully tested at the level of the nation-state to render them effective on a planetary scale.

There is another precious legacy that Europe can bring into the imminent 'civilizing process' of the planetary frontier-land. Balibar quotes from Umberto Eco the idea of the 'idiom of Europe' which has been formed in the 'practice of translation'.[38] Europe was for many centuries a composite totality, bringing many languages and cultural strands into daily contact and conversation with each other. One could say that Europe was for that reason a natural soil for hermeneutics, the art of interpretation and understanding, to flourish in. Europe has been and remains a homeland of perpetual translation; in the process, it has learned to make a fruitful dialogue between cultural and linguistic idioms effective without effacing the identity of any of the participants. It has learned (to quote Franz Rosenzweig's expression) to treat the partners in conversation as having tongues in addition to ears; as speakers, not merely listeners. Balibar suggests that this tradition-grounded practical ability of speaking/listening, teaching/learning, understanding and making oneself understood (in short, of translating) 'could also be expanded by stretching the idea of "translation" from the merely linguistic to the broader *cultural* level'. Europe may yet play a crucial role in the conception, birth and maturation of a planetary community in its capacity of 'interpreter of the world'.

Balibar dubs that role a 'vanishing mediator' (like that played according to Max Weber by the 'Protestant ethic' in the emergence of modern capitalist rationality): the success of the role would be measured by Europe working itself out of a job as the progressive 'institutionalization of conflict' and perpetual dialogue elbow out the ways and means of a frontier-land and replace the present-day Hobbesian world with Kant's humanity-wide polity. Let me comment that the 'vanishing mediator' pattern seems a much better fit for the phantom empire imagined to be currently run by the American superpower. It is that irrational creed which in the long run may well prove to have played the function of 'midwife' in the delivery of forces able to, and/or having 'no choice but to . . . ', carry out a 'Europeanization of the globe' – shaping the outlines of the planetary polity of the future.

The present-day frontier-land conditions galvanized by the phantom empire may well go down in history as the circumstance that effectively salvaged the 'European idiom' from vanishing.

# 3

## From Social State to Security State

The unnamed beast of Franz Kafka's 'The burrow' boasts that 'the real entrance' to the burrow which it has been digging for a long time, and is still digging, 'is covered by a movable layer of moss' and so 'is secured as safely as anything in this world can be secured'. And yet, it complains, 'someone could step on the moss or break through it, and then my burrow would lie open, and anybody who liked . . . could make his way in and destroy everything for good.'[1]

'Someone' . . . anyone, in fact – and there is no one outside the burrow you can really trust. It is comparatively easy to trust someone you supervise, and you may even trust someone at a distance: 'but completely to trust someone outside the burrow when you are inside the burrow, that is, in a different world, that, it seems to me, is impossible'. To make things even worse, 'there are also enemies in the bowels of the earth. I have never seen them, but legends tell of them and I firmly believe in them.' Because of those invisible enemies, 'it is of no avail to console yourself with the thought that you are in your own house; far rather are you in theirs.' In the end, when it comes to safety, the inside of the burrow is not much better than the outside, and you won't draw a clear line between the two however hard you try . . .

'The truth of the matter', muses the burrow-digger, is that 'in reality the burrow does provide a considerable degree of security, but by no means enough, for is one ever free from anxieties inside it?' 'My constant preoccupation with defensive measures involves a frequent alteration and modification.' My safety will never be total, the burrow never be complete, the job never be finished. It is only my constant 'altering and modifying' that calms, as long as it goes on, the fear. It is in the flutter and commotion of the never-ending flight to safety, in that constant digging and covering of the traces, that security can be sought (if not from the enemy, then from the anxiety the enemy causes): 'keeping one's ear fixed to the wall and at every hint of noise tearing out a lump of earth, not really hoping to find anything, but simply so as to do something to give expression to one's inward agitation'. Anxiety disturbs life, but life turns gradually into a string of disturbances; tearing that string breaks life as one has learned to live it and to recognize it as life. Life is anxiety, anxiety is life. 'I would probably like nothing better than to start stubbornly and defiantly digging, simply for the sake of digging, at some place or other, whether I heard anything there or not.'

The story is told by the animal as it nears the end of its anxiety-fighting, burrow-digging life. With life's fatigue comes life's wisdom. Old creatures are given to reminiscences, retrospection, reflection – all the more so because of their fast dwindling strength: the weaker the hands, the longer the empty moments which thoughts may and need to fill. Thoughts absolve ageing hands from the sin of sloth – this is why old creatures are often deemed both cynical and sagacious. Kafka's burrow-digger resists the push to dig more trenches: 'This trench will bring me certainty, you say? I have reached the stage where I no longer wish to have certainty.' Life without uncertainty – what would it be like?

Would it still be a life? Is not fear the very thing that makes life worth living? At the end of a lifelong fight for safety, the prospect of that safety achieved and no longer needing to be fought for is terrifying. At the end of a fear-filled life, the most awesome fear is the absence of fear.

You can hear a sigh of relief in the sentence 'But all remained unchanged' with which the hero of 'The burrow' ends his confessions – having first come to the conclusion that, all his hectic agitation notwithstanding, he would never know whether the enemy did or did not trace his shelter and what the enemy's intentions might have been. The meaning of life wouldn't survive the fear's demise. Security would sound a death-knell to meaningful life and lay bare that life's absurdity . . .

We, human beings, are inveterate meaning-seekers. One can even go as far as taking the question 'what for?' as the defining trait of humanity. Once fighting fear becomes synonymous with meaningful life, we tend to become fear-dependent; we are fear's addicts. We need a dose each day – and as in any addiction worth its name each day we need a larger dose than the day before. What we fear most is an overdose, and we fear it because we fear the end of fearing it portends. Derrida would probably count fear among the foremost specimens of *pharmacon*, the 'drug' – that medicine and poison rolled into one, a remedy when served regularly and in the right quantity, a venom if overdone, with the line separating the right dose from the wrong one shifty and impossible to pinpoint, let alone keep in one place.

No wonder fear sells, and sells well. A recent newspaper advertisement for a TV satellite giant encourages the viewers to switch on: 'What if you could catch a deadly virus by touching something? Like a newspaper . . . ' Fear addicts need more, always more, and the demand for new and improved fears is unlikely ever to wilt, let alone dry up – even if the fear industry, like all consumer-oriented industries, compensates for its failures of intelligence and hedges its bets with an excess and so tends to overshoot the target time and again.

In fear, the consumer industry has found the bottomless and self-replenishing gold-mine it has long sought. For the consumer industry, fear is a fully and truly 'renewable resource'. Fear has become the *perpetuum mobile* of the consumer market – and so of the present-day economy.

It has been mostly in Europe and its overseas offshoots, branches and sedimentary deposits that the addiction to fear and the obsession with security have made by far their most spectacular career in recent years.

In itself, this looks like a mystery. After all, as Robert Castel points out in his incisive analysis of the current insecurity-fed anxieties, 'we – at least in the developed countries – live undoubtedly in some of the most secure [*sûres*] societies that ever existed.'[2] And yet, contrary to the 'objective evidence', it is the cosseted and pampered 'we', of all people, who feel more threatened, insecure and frightened, more inclined to panic, and more passionate about everything related to security and safety than people of most other societies on record.

Sigmund Freud confronted the puzzle point-blank and suggested that its solution should be sought in the human psyche's staunch defiance of the dry 'logic of facts'. Human suffering (and so also the fear of suffering, and fear as the most vexatious and aggravating specimen of suffering) arises from the 'superior power of nature, the feebleness of our own bodies and the inadequacy of the regulations which adjust the mutual relationships of human beings in the family, the state and society'.[3]

As to the first two causes named by Freud, we manage one way or another to reconcile ourselves to the ultimate limits of what we can do: we know that we shall never fully master nature and that we cannot make our mortal bodies immortal or immune to the merciless flow of time – and so we are ready to settle for 'second best'. That knowledge, however, is stimulating and energizing rather than depressing and disabling: if we cannot remove all suffering, we can remove some kinds and mitigate others – the matter is worth trying, and trying over and over again.

It is altogether different, however, with the third kind of suffering: the misery with a *social* origin. Whatever is made by humans can be remade by humans. We do not accept any limit to such remaking – at any rate no limit that with due determination and goodwill could not be broken by human effort: 'we cannot see why the regulations made by ourselves should not . . . be a protection and a benefit for every one of us.' If the 'really available protection' and the benefits we enjoy stop short of the ideal, if the relationships are still not of our liking, if regulations are not what they should be (and, as we believe, could be), we are likely to suspect hostile machinations, plots, the conspiracy of an enemy at the gate or under the bed. Ill will in short, and a culprit, and a crime or a criminal intention.

Castel comes to a similar conclusion, when he suggests that modern insecurity does not derive from a dearth of protection, but from the 'lack of clarity of its scope' (*ombre portée*) in a social universe that 'has been organized around an unending pursuit of protection and a frantic search for security'.[4] The poignant and incurable experience of insecurity is a side-effect of the conviction that, given the right skills and proper effort, full security can be achieved (it can be done, we can do it) – and if it transpires that it has not been done, the failure can only be explained by a wicked deed and malice aforethought. Of this piece, there must be a villain.

We can say that the modern variety of insecurity is distinctively marked by the fear of malevolence and malefactors. It is shot through by suspicion of others and their intentions, and by a refusal to trust, or the impossibility of trusting, the constancy and reliability of human companionship. Castel charges modern individualization with the responsibility for such a state of affairs; he suggests that modern society, having taken away the closely knit communities and corporations which once defined the rules of protection and monitored their application, and replaced them with the individual duty of self-care and self-help, has been built on the quicksand of contingency: in such a society, insecurity and fear of diffuse danger are endemic.

As in all other modern transformations, Europe played the pioneering role here. It was also the first to confront the unanticipated and as a rule unwholesome consequences of change. This unnerving sense of insecurity would not have sprung up if it had not been for the simultaneous occurrence of two departures that occurred in Europe, spreading later, and with varying speeds, to other parts of the planet. The first was, to follow Castel's terminology, the 'overvaluation' (*survalorisation*) of the individual liberated from the constraints imposed by a dense network of social bonds.[5] But the second departure followed closely behind: an unprecedented frailty and vulnerability of the individual stripped of the protection offered in the past, and matter-of-factly, by the dense network of social bonds.

The first departure unfolded in front of individual human beings, offering exciting, seductively vast expanses for practising self-constitution and self-improvement. But the second departure barred most individuals from entry. The combined outcome of both was the salt of guilt rubbed ever anew into the permanently festering wound of impotence. The name of the resulting disease was the fear of inadequacy.

From the start, the modern state was confronted with the daunting task of the management of fear. It had to weave back the network of protection that the modern revolution tore apart, and go on repairing the net as the continuous modernization promoted by that state kept straining and fraying it. Contrary to a widespread view, it was the *protection* (collective insurance against individual ill-fortune) rather than the *redistribution of wealth* that lay at the heart of the 'social state' to which the development of the modern state unyieldingly led. For people deprived of economic, cultural or social capital (all assets other than their labouring ability), 'protection is collective or none at all.'[6]

Unlike the protective networks of the premodern past, the state-conceived and state-administered safety nets were either constructed deliberately and by design, or evolved by their own momentum out of the other large-scale constructive labours characteristic of modernity in its 'solid' phase. The welfare institutions and provisions (sometimes called 'social wages'), the state-run or state-assisted health services, schooling and housing, and factory bills spelling out the mutual rights and obligations of both sides to labour contracts, and by the same token protecting the well-being and entitlements of the employees, provide examples of the first category.

The foremost instance of the second category was factory floor, trade union and occupational solidarity that took root and flourished 'naturally' in the relatively stable environment of the 'Fordist factory', the epitome of the solid-modern setting in which most of those 'lacking other capital' were fixed. The engagement between the opposite sides of capital–labour relations was mutual and ongoing in that factory, making both sides dependent on each other but at the same time enabling them to think and plan into the long term, to bind the future and invest in it. The 'Fordist factory' was for that reason a site of bitter, sometimes boiling, but at all times simmering conflict (the long-term engagement and mutual dependency of all sides made the confrontation a reasonable investment and a sacrifice that paid off) – but it was also a secure shelter for trust and so for negotiation, compromise and a search for a consensual mode of cohabitation. With its clearly defined career tracks, tiresome but reassuringly stable routines, slow pace of change in the composition of labour teams, continuing usefulness of acquired skills and high values therefore attached to accumulated work experience, the labour market's hazards could be held at arm's length, uncertainty could be subdued if not entirely eliminated, and fears could be assigned to the marginal realm of 'blows of fate' and 'fatal accidents', rather than saturating the run of daily life. Above all, those many who missed out on all capital but their labour could count on collectivity. Solidarity reforged the ability to labour into a substitute capital – and a kind of capital that it was hoped, not without reason, would counterbalance the combined power of all other kinds of capital.

Modern fears were born during the first bout of deregulation-cum-individualization, at the moment when the kinship and neighbourly bonds between people, apparently eternal or at least present since time immemorial, tightly tied into community or corporation knots, were loosened or broken. The solid-modern mode of fear management tended to replace the irreparably damaged 'natural' bonds with their artificial equivalents in the form of associations, unions and part-time yet quasi-permanent collectives unified by shared daily routines; *solidarity* took over from *belonging* as the main shield against an increasingly hazardous fate.

The dissipation of solidarity spelled the end of the solid-modern fashion of fear management. The turn has now come for the modern, artificial, administered protections to be loosened, dismantled or otherwise broken. Europe, the first to undergo the modern overhaul and the first to run the whole spectrum of its sequels, is now going through 'deregulation-cum-individualization mark two' – though this time not of its own choice, but succumbing to the pressure of global forces it can no longer control or hope to check.

Paradoxically, the more that is left locally of the 'cradle to grave' protections now everywhere under assault, the more attractive become xenophobic outlets for the gathering feelings of imminent danger. The few (mostly Scandinavian) countries that are still reluctant to abandon the institutionalized protections left from solid-modern times, fighting back the multiple pressures to reduce them or disband them altogether, view themselves as fortresses besieged by enemy forces. They consider the remnants of the social state as a privilege that needs to be defended, tooth and nail, against intruders eager to plunder them or further dilute them and thin them out. Xenophobia, the growing suspicion of a foreign plot and resentment of 'strangers' (mostly of migrants, those vivid and highly visible reminders that walls can be pierced and borders effaced, natural effigies, asking to be burned, of mysterious globalizing forces running out of control), can be seen as a perverse reflection of desperate attempts to salvage whatever remains of local solidarity.

Once competition replaces solidarity, individuals find themselves abandoned to their own, pitifully meagre and evidently inadequate resources. The dilapidation and decomposition of collective bonds made them, without asking their consent, into individuals *de jure* – but overwhelming and intractable odds militate against their rise to the postulated model of individuals *de facto*.[7] If under solid-modern conditions the most feared individual misfortune was the failure to conform, now – in the wake of the liquid modern turn – the most frightening spectre is inadequacy. It is a well-founded apprehension, to be sure, considering the yawning gap that separates the quantity and quality of resources required by an effective production of a do-it-yourself but nonetheless reliable and trustworthy security, from the sum total of materials, tools and skills which the majority of individuals can reasonably hope to acquire and retain.

Robert Castel also signals the return of *dangerous classes*.[8] Let us observe, though, that the similarity between their first and their second appearance is partial at best.

The original 'dangerous classes' were made up of the temporarily excluded and not-yet reintegrated population surplus which accelerating economic progress deprived of a 'useful function', while the accelerating pulverization of bond networks stripped them of protection. The new 'dangerous classes', on the other hand, are those recognized as unfit for reintegration and proclaimed unassimilable, since no useful function can be conceived that they could perform after 'rehabilitation'. They are not just excessive, but *redundant*. They are excluded *permanently* – one of the few cases of 'permanence' which liquid modernity not only allows, but actively promotes. Rather than being perceived as the outcome of a momentary and repairable bad luck, today's exclusion exudes an air of finality. More and more, exclusion today tends to be a one-way street. Bridges once burnt are unlikely ever to be rebuilt. It is the irrevocability of their eviction and the dimness of their chances of appealing against the verdict that makes the contemporary excluded into 'dangerous classes'.

The irrevocability of exclusion is a direct, though unforeseen consequence of the decomposition of the social state – as a web of established institutions, but perhaps even more significantly as an ideal and a project. The emaciation, decline and breakdown of the latter portend, after all, the disappearance of redemptive opportunities and the withdrawal of the right to appeal, and so also the gradual dissipation of hope and the wilting of any will to resist. Rather than as a condition of 'un-employment' (the term implying a departure from the norm, a temporary affliction that can and shall be cured), being out of a job feels increasingly like a state of 'redundancy' – being rejected, branded as superfluous, useless, unemployable and doomed to remain 'economically inactive'. Being out of a job implies being disposable, perhaps even disposed of already and once and for all – assigned to the waste of 'economic progress', that change which boils down in the last account to doing the same work and achieving the same economic results but with a smaller workforce and less in 'labour costs' than before.

Only a thin line today separates the unemployed, and especially the long-term unemployed, from a fall into the black hole of the 'underclass': men and women not fitting into any legitimate social division, individuals left outside classes and carrying none of the recognized, approved, useful and indispensable functions the 'normal' members of society perform – people who add nothing to the life of society except what society could well do without and would gain from getting rid of. Just as tenuous is the line separating the 'redundant' from criminals: the 'underclass' and 'criminals' are but two subcategories of 'anti-social elements', differing from each other more by the official classification and the treatment they receive than by their own stance and conduct. Just like the people out of a job, criminals (that is, those consigned to prison, charged or under police supervision, or simply on police registers) are no longer viewed as temporarily evicted from normal social life and bound to be 're-educated', 'rehabilitated' and 'returned to the community' at the earliest opportunity – but as permanently marginalized, unfit for 'social recycling' and bound to be kept out of mischief for the duration, away from the community of the law-abiding.

The outlets for the disposal of 'redundant humans' are no longer available. For centuries, modernizing Europe used to unload overseas the surplus population made superfluous by technological and economic progress at home – seeking and finding 'global' solutions to locally generated social problems. Today, however, while the production of 'human waste' goes on unabated in the developed countries of Europe and the rest of the Western world, the waste-disposal industry, another modern invention, is in deep crisis: dumping sites away from home have become scarce and are shrinking fast. Places considered empty or underpopulated have now started to produce their own population surpluses; they intermittently put their own redundant youngsters into soldier's uniforms with a brief to force back some neighbouring peoples in order to gain more space for themselves, while other youngsters stay in civilian clothes and are sent to faraway countries with instructions to support their families left behind by sending them the money they are expected to earn out there, but would not if they stayed at home. For the lack of an alternative, the 'underclass' and the rapidly growing prison-and-detention industry must absorb the locally produced 'wasted humans' that overseas lands, no longer the sites of European colonization, will not soak off; and the increasingly thinly spread social assistance funds are in danger of being further diluted by the victims of the economic progress taking off on other continents – which the nascent authorities are neither allowed nor willing to bail out from their misery.

Pressed/forced as they continuously are – by the joint forces of global banks and trading corporations supported by the International Monetary Fund and sometimes assisted by expeditionary military forces equipped for 'regime change' – to open up their borders to world markets and give up all hope of stemming foreign buy-outs code-named 'free competition', former colonies are in no position to adopt the strategy undertaken in the past by the pioneers of modernization, notably by Europe: the strategy that led eventually to the emergence of the social state. Markets, says Benjamin R. Barber, 'can bleed through porous national boundaries and are not any more constrained by the logic of sovereignty than are SARS, crime, or terrorism'.[9] The privatization of national assets (or of the assets that could become national wealth, were they not auctioned away to the highest or most formidable bidder before being given the chance of doing so) which the IMF and the World Bank have made the condition of any financial assistance and the Pentagon has made the condition of immunity from 'regime change' does not, of course, help to 'privilege the power of a common will and public good over the anarchy of private power'; on the contrary, it 'celebrates private power unencumbered by law, regulations, or government' and thereby 'reverses the traditional logic of social contract thinking on which America was founded' and which Europe until recently followed, even if by fits and starts, throughout its modern history.

The chance to unload locally produced surplus population in distant parts of the globe, the chance that offered a safety valve to a modernizing Europe as long as the modern economy remained an exquisitely European privilege, is not available to lands that are drawn into the modernizing treadmill today. Countries that once exported their massive labour surpluses would not now throw their doors open to their import. They still need an influx of cheap labour to do dirty, poorly paid and

onerous jobs in certain branches of the economy like
construction, catering, public transport or hotels, so the
doors cannot be locked entirely; but entry is strictly con-
trolled. When David Blunkett, the British Home Secretary, declares (not without a lot of pressure from
industrialists hungry for cheap, obedient and 'flexible'
labour) that 'we need legal, managed economic migration', he immediately adds: of the kind required by our
economy.[10] And to leave no doubt that no humane motives are involved and no 'universal human rights' figure in
the treatment of the disinherited, and that the 'require-
ments of our economy' are and will remain the sole con-
sideration, he hurries on to announce that the benefits of
the social state won't be made available to the new immigrants, and that the number of applications for asylum
will fall further thanks to tougher treatment applied to
unwanted and rejected asylum seekers – such as detention
camps and forced transportation to their country of origin
or to refugee camps in third countries.

Alain Morice sums up the most recent shifts in European
policy towards refugees from the impoverished and conflict-ridden South – exemplified by Dutch parliamentary
approval for a decision to deport 26,000 asylum seekers
from countries like Chechnya, Afghanistan or Somalia – as
the 'death and burial of the right to asylum' (agreed and
almost universally endorsed in 1951).[11] There is a total,
coordinated retreat from the promise that people whose
lives are in danger will be granted safety on the grounds of
their right to live; the difference between the treatment
accorded to asylum seekers and that visited on 'mere economic migrants' has been all but effaced. The tendency
today is towards paying selected third countries in other
continents to establish camps where potential asylum
seekers will be detained before they manage to reach any
European destination (as they keep trying to do against

rising odds: in the last ten years, more than 4,000 have died in the process, drowned after sailing on unseaworthy ships where they were being carried at exorbitant prices, or suffocated in sealed trucks or in their false-bottom compartments). That move towards confining refuge-seekers in camps safely distant from any place where they could start a new life has been pioneered by the government of Great Britain, which gives the camps the misleading and perhaps duplicitous name of 'transit processing centres', but the idea has immediately caught the imagination of other European governments. It follows from the public declaration of Ruud Lubbers, the UN High Commissioner for Refugees, in November 2003 that, rather than the protection of individuals and groups in danger and assisting their resettlement, his major brief and major concern was now the facilitating of the efforts of European governments to 'delocalize' potential asylum seekers, to deport them or prevent them from entering Europe.

We may say that the new planetary empire, run and administered by global capital and trade, wages 'pre-emptive strikes' daily against any budding 'social contract thinking' in the post-colonial world. The flip side of the wholesale privatization of profits and assets is the need to stave off any possible resistance against the enforced precarization of individual fate. In the last account, the policy pursued by the international institutions of free trade prevents the establishment of a public sphere where individual choices could congeal into public choices, citizenship and democratic self-government could take root, and the principles and institutions of collective protection against individually suffered risks could be negotiated into political practice.

In short, the deeds of the planetary empire belie its words. The deeds undermine, perhaps even eradicate, the self-same chances of democracy in whose name, ostensibly, the economic arm of the empire ploughs the remaining virgin lands of the planet, while the military arm polices the lands where shoots of resistance to the predatory exploitation of local resources may be suspected. Both arms cooperate in making sure that a 'social state' is not an option. But if a social state is not an option, what is the alternative?

Instead of sowing the seeds of democracy, both imperial arms are busy planting dictatorial and corrupt yet pliable governments, and starving, incapacitating and uprooting all others. The planet is spattered today by warlords' fiefs, strong-men's estates and 'no states'. In all such places the rulers' rule is reduced mostly to diverting to private coffers whatever assets have been spared by global predators and have not yet been destroyed by domestic warfare. For the ruled, this situation portends thorough incapacitation, material poverty and no hope of improvement. It also means the daily misery of a hazardous and precarious existence and of perpetual fear; a fragile life that can be denied or made invalid at any moment. For youngsters with a prospect of life without prospects, enlisting in the service of one or another of the warring chiefs, joining one of the competing armed gangs or entering one of the improvised military (terrorist) training camps are the sole realistic chances of 'life careers', and indeed of a meaningful life – or at least of a meaningful death.

Elsewhere, religious communities step in to deputize for the stillborn or aborted social state. They offer protection and solidarity, the social state's most appealing promises, though unlike the social state they offer belonging, sameness and conformity as the prime warrants of safety. They provide a 'security in numbers', of a crowd or swarm kind, instead of the safety net with which the designers of the social state and welfare protection hoped to encourage freedom of movement, individual liberty of judgement and action, and the courage to take risks. It is of course too early to tell whether the present-day religious fundamentalism, gathering in attractiveness and influence in the absence of the other, secular protections against the hazards of life in the global casino, will appear in retrospect to be a greenhouse of individualistic life philosophies and strategies similar to those which the European social state was instrumental in promoting. (Did not Puritan fundamentalism prove to be, as Max Weber famously suggested but the Puritan prophets could not possibly predict, an overture to modern capitalism's self-centred, egotistic rationality?) In the short run, though, present-day religious fundamentalism, acting against the powerful tide of market-promoted individualism, is more likely to usher in a period of ossifying dogmas, sharpening doctrinal antagonisms, Manichean worldviews and religious wars.

For the time being, the overall results of tearing up the traditional protective networks and preventing the design-and-build of their replacements is the growing insecurity of the planet; the whole of the planet, to be sure, because of the intimate interdependence of all parts of the globe and its inhabitants.

The combination of really existing or hoped-for and planned-for full employment with a dense network of state-administered protections against the vagaries of individual fate during the 'glorious thirty' years of postwar Europe resulted in a generalized feeling of social stability and individual security. The grounds for such a feeling and so also for the trust in a secure future (barring a nuclear holocaust, of course) was, as Philippe Robert recently pointed out, an 'insecurity stopper' ('bloqueur d'insécurité'),[12] with collectively guaranteed access to almost all the essential amenities – accommodation, means of transport, health services and schooling – coinciding with the advent of mass consumption. One could of course argue that the price of such security was anything but modest: work was routinized and on the whole dull and unexciting, wages were kept on the low side and rose only slowly – but 'one could rent lodging, marry, buy a vehicle on credit' and otherwise plan one's life 'long term' without fearing a sudden catastrophe that could destroy the family's well-being overnight.

Job security supplied a particularly nourishing food for trust in future: legally protected collective labour contracts, further strengthened by the bargaining impact of the threat to withdraw labour under conditions of near-full employment and the relative immobility of capital investments, prompted both sides to seek, negotiate and observe a *modus coexistendi* that would proffer the long-term security they both needed and craved. 'We are hardly disposed now', observes Richard Sennett, 'to think of routinized time as a personal *achievement*, but given the stresses, booms, and depressions of industrial capitalism, it often becomes so . . . Routine can demean, but it can also protect; routine can decompose labour, but it can also compose a life.'[13]

Robert dates the end of the 'glorious thirty years' and the times of blissful unconcern about life risks at midway through the 1970s. It was then that the issue of 'insecurity' leapt into public awareness as if from nowhere, losing no time in settling at the centre of public debate. Deregulation of the global movement of capital and of the labour market had just started. Its immediate effect was to bring protracted, probably chronic and on the whole prospectless unemployment, a frailty or absence of labour contracts, employment for a fixed term or terminated on demand, flexible labour hours and unfixed wages. After a few decades of what must have appeared in retrospect as blissful security, the new labour order (or rather the sudden chaos) must have come as a blow that shattered the world as 'people without capital other than their labour' knew it. Exclusion was no longer felt as a moment-ary stumble, but as a durable, perhaps even permanent condition – and the authorities reinforced that impression by a frightening change in the vocabulary of their program-matic pronouncements: from the elimination and preven-tion of exclusion to the containment and management of the excluded.

An amazing finding made by Robert is of a relatively low level of violent crime at a time when fear of violence and preoccupation with security surged upwards. Records show that the volume of violent acts started rising quite a few years *after* public opinion regarded its ubiquity and swelling mass as 'self-evident' and settled it as a public *doxa*. Focusing anxiety on areas populated mostly by recent immigrants and, by common consent, teeming with criminals and breeding violence came later still – but the way was well prepared by the years of existential earthquake, and its progress followed closely the ongoing phasing-out of the collective, institutionalized protection of individual lives. Anxiety was desperately seeking a cap-acious, expeditious and credible outlet. Putting two and two together, associating the new unfamiliar sentiment of wobbliness and frailty about one's familiar place in the world with a new unfamiliar sight of strangely looking and strangely behaving crowds filling the familiar streets was an almost natural, obvious step to take.

It was not only those at the bottom end of the new 'stratification by degree of individual security' who were overwhelmed by anxiety seeking an outlet – not only the unskilled labourers already exposed to the vagaries of a 'flexible', deregulated labour market offering only brittle, volatile and eminently unreliable jobs. The spectre of 'disposability', the awareness of a fast-shrinking distance between any apparently solid standing in the world and a denial of function leading to an assignment to waste, must have haunted all and sundry: those still ostensibly secure as much as those already cast out. The tides of 'precarization' inundated the whole range of social locations, from top to bottom, from the most conspicuously privileged to the most grossly deprived – though of course the statistical odds of exclusion and its depth go up the lower down the starting point of a career is placed.

In Jacques Donzelot's opinion there is nowadays no line separating the included from the (potentially) excluded, and most certainly no tight and impermeable (secure!) border keeping the two categories apart. 'Inclusion' and 'exclusion' are rather two poles of a smooth continuum along which the life itineraries of all men and women are plotted, and along which their trajectories vacillate – erratically and unpredictably. 'The excluded', says Donzelot, 'represent only the extremity, a sort of the final stage of the movement of desegregation that starts at the centre though it affects most strongly those on periphery.'[14] Exclusion has become a realistic prospect for virtually everyone, and everyone must be prepared to cope with the resulting anxiety.

Given the variety of available resources, the ways of tackling anxiety differ. People for whom the eventuality of exclusion is for the time being just a nightmare, not yet faced when wide-awake, may try to repress the thought by territorial separation from those already afflicted: keeping their distance – at home, in the office and on the way from one to the other – from those already struck and smitten, the walking reminders of a universally shared jeopardy. The people from whom they try to stay at a distance don't have such a luxury, though. It is their streets that take the full blow of the exclusionary storms, and no insulation tape or patented locks, even CCTV, could manage to protect the gates of their homes.

The shakiness and unpredictability of the settings in which livings are made are probably the most prolific sources of anguish, but not its only sources. The new vulnerability and frailty of human bonds[15] are another powerful reason to worry and fear for the future. There are few if any cloudless moments, free from premonition, when flitting or dashing through one's 'network' directory or kneading the mini-keyboard of a mobile. Partnerships are eminently and imminently breakable, commitments are revocable and amenable to unsolicited termination at any time, telephone numbers may go dead and calls remain stubbornly unanswered, and heartless snubs may replace the joyful welcomes to which one has become accustomed and come, gullibly, to treat as owed by right. Scanning the network is like skating on smoothly polished ice: exhilarating on a rink visited at weekends, but calling for full, no-rest-allowed and so increasingly tiresome vigilance if it is turned into the sole available surface for daily walks.

However awesome such reasons are for being nervous and afraid, they are but the beginning of a long list of sources of anxiety. With seduction (always fleeting, always in cut-throat competition with other baits and allures) elbowing out normative regulations, and the excitement of awakening new and untested desires replacing the monotony of keeping the old and boringly familiar needs satisfied, there is little time left to pause, relax and count one's blessings. It is (transient) *appropriation* that counts, not (durable) *possession*; prompt and timely disposal, not safekeeping and preservation. One never knows what one will need to desire tomorrow and when the objects of today's desire will lose their lustre. What matters is pricking one's ears to hear the first signals of the new 'coming in' and the old 'falling out'; staying on the track rather than running its whole length, since the finishing line is either absent or moves faster than the fastest of runners. Again, the life of a runner may be enjoyable (or at least that is what we've managed to convince ourselves is true), but it certainly is exhausting. The price is the fear, never put to rest, of stumbling, getting out of breath, falling off the track altogether.

The list of fears is like the consumerist trajectory – unfinished and in all probability unfinishable. Fear capital from which economic and political profits can be drawn is, for all practical intents and purposes, unlimited.

A few weeks ago TV screens were full of people crowding the lobbies of airports, waiting for days for their planes to be allowed to fly, and for hours to reach the X-ray and interview booths, to be sniffed all over by police dogs before boarding the plane – watched all the time by heavily armed guards. Swarms of the presumed guilty, each waiting to prove her or his individual innocence.

In our times of public confessions it wouldn't be good television unless the reporters picked out faces from the faceless crowd – male and female faces, young and old – and asked those people how they felt . . . And so the reporters did what reporters are supposed to do, and asked: 'Aren't you furious to be kept away from your nearest and dearest? To miss your business meeting? To spend your holiday time watching departure boards and lining up for checks?' 'Oh no, on the contrary! We are delighted and grateful,' so the answers went, all the answers, unanimous answers, choral answers rehearsed singly over and over again, all the way from soprano to bass. 'What a relief! We've never felt so secure. Those in charge of our security are really doing their jobs.'

So far, nothing new. Many years before Charles Lindbergh pioneered transatlantic flights and still more years before fingernail files were first X-rayed in grandmothers' handbags and triumphantly confiscated at the checkouts of airports, a tale circulated through Eastern Europe of a devout follower of the great Rabbi of Zhitomir who was trying to convince a doubting Thomas of the unearthly powers of his saintly mentor and how his omnipotence was second to none. 'The Jews of Kiev sent a deputation to the Rabbi to complain that their city was teeming with anti-Semites and to ask him to do something about it,' he said. 'To help the Jews, the Rabbi prayed to God and asked him to burn the villains' den down – and God, as always, consented. The deputies were, however, taken aback by the swiftness, severity and wholesale nature of the response. They pointed out to the Rabbi that some nice people, of which even the infested city had a few, might also be scorched in the fire. So the Rabbi prayed again, this time begging God not to let Kiev go up in smoke.' 'And can't you see,' shouted the Hassid ecstatically, 'no one was burnt, no house was gutted, Kiev is still sound and whole!' The tale ended – your guess is right – with the conversion of the sceptic.

So what is new, apart from replacing rabbis with state-run or commercial security companies, prayers with CCTV, X-rays, sniffer dogs and fingerprinting, and Hassids with tabloid editorial and story writers? At the time when the above tale circled the little towns of Eastern Europe, Karl Marx suggested that history occurs twice, first as a tragedy and the second time as a farce; in this case, however, the sequence has been reversed. The joke has turned uncannily real; the grotesque has turned into a tragedy.

A good part of the R&D funds of marketing giants is earmarked for the production of consumers. There would be no point in spending company money on the invention of 'new and improved' consumer goods were there no consumers to covet and yearn for them, ready to spend their money on their share of the first batch and to queue for hours on end for the privilege. The new goods arouse the consumers' zeal because they promise to deliver what the consumers need – but would the consumers know what they needed and where to turn to to get it if they were not properly enlightened? They probably wouldn't; they would have no inkling of what they *really* needed, and of course they would not have the slightest idea of what kind of implement or service was the best for gratifying their need.

Of course, even the most ingenious spin doctors could not conjure up a totally new need out of nothing. Rather, they must capitalize on a craving, an uneasiness or a worry that is already felt, though for the time being in a 'raw' form, as yet unprocessed but eminently 'processable': an inarticulate tension as yet unnamed, still diffuse and unfocused. The less definite the vaguely felt disquiet, the better. Spin doctors like their 'raw material' to be vague and shapeless, flexible, submissive, soft and kneadable, ready to take up many shapes – so that it can be given that specific form which the suppliers of goods are eager to serve or credibly claim to be serving. Their role boils down to 'only connect'. It consists in condensing the foggy and scattered anxieties into a need with a name, and then representing whatever the markets currently have to offer as the right answer to that need. The same anxieties may be remoulded to respond to different offers – and they are indeed repeatedly recycled. Once a particular offer is for whatever reason withdrawn, the previously established connection must be severed and the loose strings tied in a different knot.

Arguably the most conspicuous among the offers presently withdrawn from the 'political market' is that of the social state; at loggerheads with the consumer market logic, it fell, unsurprisingly, as the first casualty of the retreat of the state from the normative regulation of business enterprise. The consumer market thrives on the same fear capital which the state when it was aiming to become a social state promised to eradicate; it is mainly for that reason that everything directly or obliquely related to the philosophy and practice of the 'social state' is, for the philosophers and practitioners of the consumer market, an anathema. The success of the social state spells the stagnation or demise of the market, and so the social state is the first obstacle that market forces have to move out of the way of their own success.

Escape from fear is the best 'selling point'. Nothing sells like anti-fear contraptions, and the most salient symptom of the passage of power from the state to the market is the policy of cutting taxes, a policy whose bottom line is the shifting back to the market of the funds previously drawn into state coffers to finance socially provided individual security; in different words, the 'commercialization of fear' – a massive transfer of the resource named 'fear' from the governance of political power to that of market players. It is that resource which was 'deregulated' and 'privatized' in the first place. It is now up to the consumer market to capitalize on the otherwise unattended fear. And it does – with gusto and ever rising skills.

Be it the magic spray exterminating carpet mites invisible to the naked eye and for that reason particularly frightening, bleaches with secret ingredients guaranteed to destroy 'the dirt you see and the dirt you don't', sticky tape to seal windows against anthrax terrorists, TV cameras to keep away strangers oozing unspecified dangers, organic foods that protect against the pedlars of poisoned and/or poisoning food, and diet foods that starve and destroy bodily fat, their fifth column, or SUVs – personal armed cars with battering rams instead of buffers to keep off the lesser 'drivers from hell', with reassuringly thick steel plates to keep at bay the danger-saturated 'outside' – when it comes to grazing on human anxieties and channelling human fears to profitable uses, the inventiveness of the marketing promoters knows no limits. And there is always the last, unencroachable line of trenches: the fear of being found with yesterday's devices meant to parry the day-before-yesterday's fears . . .

The rapidly developing 'security industry', the one industry where prospects of redundancy stay comfortably remote and which can justly claim to do what it preaches, that is to be secure, may well be the principal beneficiary of the dismantling of the social state. Prompted on 30 January 2004 to find websites referring to security, Google returned (in 0.14 seconds) about 66,400,000 entries. It took Lycos a fraction of a second longer to return 91,266,444, while Alltheweb found as many as 95,635,722. Given the degree of the internet's commercialization, offers of wondrous contraptions meant to enhance security of the body or the possessions of their purchasers commanded, as expected, the lion's share of those numbers. The sole 'security concern' that the state may still claim to be its monopolistic property (as once, in Max Weber's time, it claimed the monopolistic possession and management of the means of enforcement) – the terrorism and the war against it – occupied by comparison a minute (though by no means inconsiderable in its own right) share of the world wide web of information. Google listed 5,190,000 sites, Altavista 8,614,569, and Lycos came first this time with 9,011,981.

Having abandoned the ambition and withdrawn the promise to free its subjects from fears emanating from the hazards of life, the state can no longer avail itself of the legitimation it deployed for a greater part of modern history to justify its demand for its subjects' submission to law and order. Effective protection from the random blows delivered by ruthless and unconstrained market competition is simply not on and cannot be credited to the state – neither as an achievement nor as a credible prospect. Any attempt to do so, nevertheless, is likely to trigger a devastating riposte from global capital, and the adverse effects would ultimately be blamed on the incompetence of those who did it, and therefore held against the state as proof of its miscalculated 'economic policy'. As a result of the fast and relentless shrinking of the realm of the state's sovereign decisions, the 'legitimation crisis' signalled by Jürgen Habermas more than two decades ago has deepened continuously over the years and seems now to have reached a point of no return.

When democracies face a time of crisis (like the legitimation crisis of our days), Eugen Weber suggests that

> diffuse discontent and fear can focus on the Others, denounced for taking work from the natives, bread from their mouths, security from their streets, and taxes from their pockets. In such times, people who live as neighbours turn into enemies; casual nationalism veers into a xenophobic *us* against *them*. Normally immigrants are first denigrated and marginalized, but then integrated and assimilated. In hard times, however, latent antipathy turns to overt resentment and hatred, as in the great depression, when the Dutch, Belgian, Swiss, British, French and Americans set to restricting immigration. The rights of man are only what some men concede to others . . . Democracy is likely to express the prejudices of the majority as well as its better sentiments and aspirations.[16]

A frantic search for an alternative legitimation that could ride the adverse tides instead of being swept away by them took states into the area where the marketeers of consumer goods, quicker to sense new and profitable opportunities, had already wandered *en masse*: that of personal safety. Since the area was already crowded, tightly packed with merchandisers, the challenge was to carve out, or to add a sector which the state organs could credibly claim as their own monopolistic domain; the kind of threat to safety as would need the unique prerogatives of the state to be realistically fought back against, contained or eliminated. The exclusive and uncontested role of the state authorities in confronting the new edition of security threats was sought, as Jo Goodey has pointed out, through the 'fusing of immigration and crime issues into an internal security continuum' and linking 'long established demonization of the "other", in the form of the criminal threat posed to the EU by undesirable "outsiders", and increasing pressures for migration into the EU from outside', that allowed 'for an easy marriage between crime concerns and migration concerns'.[17]

Through that fusion and that marriage, the state has acquired a priceless asset in its struggle for a substitute legitimation. The opportunities for spectacular displays of state activity (and indeed of the state's indispensability) were already ample in this area, but in addition they could be multiplied at will. A lot of public attention can easily be drawn to governmental efforts to set apart 'genuine' from 'bogus' refugees or asylum seekers and to screening potential 'welfare scroungers' and mafiosi out of those who have been allowed, after high-tech scrutiny and a meticulous selection procedure, into the country. On the top of that, as Rory Carroll has observed, 'by closing virtually all legal methods of entry, Europe has ensured that outsiders have no choice but to try the trafficker. He sets a price based on demand, cost and risk. Europe's strategy is to make that cost and risk as high as possible.'[18] Vast new expanses of crime are thereby conjured up, giving governments a lot to do in order to protect the threatened safety of their citizens. The 'migration-crime-security' continuum (Goodey's phrase) allows the states of Europe to find their powerful new legitimation in the new blend of policing and immigration policies.

September 11 opened up another, even more commodious space for the construction of the new legitimation. The very size of that space is enormous, but the new space also has other advantages which a focusing of safety apprehensions on refugees does not have.

Despite their precarious position on the brink of extraterritoriality (read: outside the realm of law), refugees can still (at least in principle) appeal to 'human rights', however imprecise such rights may be, and sometimes successfully resort to the courts, local or supranational, and to the legal procedures available to the settled inhabitants of the country of their arrival. There are limits at which even the most ingenious initiatives of the authorities, eager to be seen as flexing their muscles, must stop. At the end of the day, the evidence of a link between immigration and criminality must be presented and that guilt by association must be proved, however long that end is delayed by the coalition of successive tabloid horror stories and government-sponsored panics. Refugees, like other human beings, may count on being presumed innocent until proved guilty – and so they are not perfect candidates for (to invoke Giorgio Agamben's concept) 'homini sacri' status – a status outside all legally recognized statuses, a condition stripped of all habitual meanings and one to which neither human nor divine laws apply.

Terrorists, on the other hand, can be placed openly and explicitly outside the realm of humanity: physically – in Guantanamo Bay or Bagram camp and their less publicized replicas, places fully and truly, indisputably extra

territorial and sealed off from any territorially bound juris-
diction, sites over which no established juridical system
may claim sovereignty and to which none of the rules that
have come to be seen as indispensable ingredients of
human rights allow the inmates to challenge the charges
and to attempt to prove their innocence or complain about
inhuman treatment. The intention to commit a terrorist
act is by definition tantamount to proof of inhumanity, and
standing accused of such an intention is (in practice if not
in theory) all the evidence needed that treatment reserved
for members of the human race does not apply. When they
focus public fears on the threat of terrorism, and public
concern on the 'war against terrorism', the powers-that-be
acquire a freedom of manoeuvre unavailable and unimaginable in the case of any alternative, genuine or putative, public enemy. In no other case can the state be
virtually free from apprehension that representing itself
as the sole barrier standing between its subjects and untold
as well as unspeakable horrors might be unmasked as
'sexed up', blown out of all proportion, or downright
duplicitous. In no other case can the state in its role of
law enforcer be similarly sure that its subjects will be
inclined to take the *non-realization* of dangers for proof of
their reality and of the blessed, saviour-like role of the state
security organs who warned of their imminence. 'Terror
suspects could be convicted on the evidence of "electronic
eavesdropping" of phone calls and emails under sweeping
moves to combat the threat of an al-Qaeda atrocity', states
the *Observer* of 22 February 2004. This is not all, though:
new anti-terrorism powers for government 'would see suspects convicted on lower standards of proof than in the
criminal courts, and of crimes not yet even committed,
such as an intent to execute a suicide bombing'.

As we have seen before, it is not easy to prove or disprove the size and gravity of risks; this difficulty is now

swept away by a simple enough expedient of admitting (unspecified) 'lower' standards of proof 'that these people' (the suspects guilty of morbid intentions gleaned from their telephone conversations) 'are a risk'. Since risks are in our times, by common consent, ubiquitous (as are the potential carriers of risk), such a departure opens a virtually boundless vista for present and future power-assisted factories of fear. The problem is no longer whether the accused are guilty or innocent and whether official warnings are correct, fraudulent or massaged, but whether the official definition of the affair, resting on undisclosed and admittedly undisclosable evidence, can or cannot be independently scrutinized, tested and vindicated or questioned. The dosage of public anxiety now depends more on the fighters of terrorists than on the terrorists themselves; and so it may be determined more by the political needs of governments that are impotent to bridle economic turbulence than by the scale of the damage the terrorists would dearly wish, and are able, to perpetrate.

No sane person can deny the reality of the terrorist threat. As long as our shared planetary home remains as chaotic and the global powers as unbridled and free from politics and ethical guidance, and our paroxysmal responses to terrorist outrages as one-sided, privatized and deregulated as they are now as a result of one-sided, privatized and deregulated globalization, that threat will remain real. Extraterritorial terrorism is as much an inevitable product of the way the globalization of human planetary interdependence proceeds as are extraterritorial finances and trade, crime and corruption; it will only vanish if the 'new world disorder' vanishes too – its homeland and its playground, and an inexhaustible source of its ever renewed strength.

Reacting to the Spanish response to the terrorist outrage in Madrid, the American Secretary of State for Defense reached for a parable of neighbours deciding whether or not to join in a chase of local evildoers who are a mortal threat to them all. The tacit assumption was that the American-led assault on Afghanistan and Iraq and *a priori* similar assaults that may be American-led in the future are the genuine and only proper chase, and those who suspect the assaults to be misbegotten, counterproductive and wide off the mark, and seek other, more effective ways of fighting terrorism, are by the same token opting out of the 'war against terrorism'. But Rumsfeld's parable, and the assumption it obliquely presented as allegedly self-evident, as well as most commentaries that followed the socialist victory in the Spanish elections – which assumed that the possible withdrawal of Spanish occupying forces from Iraq was tantamount to washing one's hands of the fight against terrorists – were but another symptom of a dangerously twisted discursive agenda. Contrary to what the parable suggests, the true point of contention is not whether the effort to annihilate the terrorist is a duty of Europe as much as it is of the US, but whether the 'war on terrorism' which America wants Europe to join is the right form which such an effort should take.

The real choice is between keeping the planet fertile for terrorism by perpetuating and exacerbating its free-for-all, frontier-land conditions, or reforming the planet in a way that would render the seeds of terrorism unlikely to take root and sprout (though humans being what they are, no conceivable reform will eliminate the threat of terrorist acts completely). The real 'war against terrorism' would be a concerted effort to make the planet hospitable to humanity and so inhospitable to its enemies. Such a 'war', however, would require much more than sending planes to bomb Iraq, Afghanistan or any number of other selected targets; it is by no means certain, moreover, that those deciding on strategy would consider sending the planes the right way for the fight to proceed. And judged by its effects to date, the suspicion that Rumsfeld's strategy diverts us from the declared purpose of the 'war against terrorism', instead of bringing the objective of planet-wide peaceful human coexistence closer, is all but well founded.

If the purpose of Al-Qaeda was to make the West live in fear and lose its ability to maintain its standards of freedom, justice, democracy and human dignity (all those values which the Al-Qaeda leaders and their followers have been repeatedly, and correctly, accused of the intention to destroy), it seems to have advanced towards its goal further than it could have dreamed of by its own forces. The acrid comment made on guerrilla warfare by Robert Taber, the American fighting on Castro's side at Playa Giron, has been confirmed, and in a particularly sinister form, in the case of the present-day tide of terrorist outrages: the guerrilla (or the terrorists) fight the war of the flea, and their military enemy suffers the dog's disadvantages: too much to defend; too small, ubiquitous and agile an enemy to come to grips with . . .

Once the 'war on terrorism', Rumsfeld's version, is waged, little is left to the military hunters of terrorists except to follow another pungent observation, by the great Roman historian Cornelius Tacitus: they make a wilderness and call it peace. It is the wilderness they make that renders the prospect of peace so distant and so apparently nebulous.

# 4

## *Towards a World Hospitable to Europe*

'What does Europe need strength for?' asks Tzvetan Todorov. And answers: to defend a certain identity which the Europeans think is worth defending.[1]

What, however, could that 'identity' be (that something, as Paul Ricoeur suggested, which makes its carrier recognizably different from all others while at the same time rendering it recognizably similar to itself despite the passage of time)? A special, uncommon form of life, perhaps unique so far, a way of living together, of relating to each other and availing oneself of each other's presence, by which Europeans tend to measure the propriety/decency of the world by which they are made while making it; a form of life which they struggle, with mixed success, to practise. As I argued at the beginning of this book, one of the most conspicuous features of European identity was always the tendency to run after identity, while it stays stubbornly well ahead of its pursuers.

What is 'worth defending' (as well as worth fighting for, and once possessed not easy to part with) is called 'value'. Tell me what your values are, and I'll tell you what your 'identity' is. In the case of Europe, always struggling to come nearer to a state it believed to be good and desirable, rather than settling for the state it was in (let alone failing to ask how good that latter state was and so failing to find out just how much it left to be desired), the link between values and identity is arguably still more intimate than in other cases: identity is more fully defined by the values Europeans cherish than by any other of their characteristics.

Todorov, well placed to do the job thanks to a biography that spanned both sides of what some people view as Europe's outer frontier – while some others see it as Europe's two-millennia-old yet now outdated 'great divide' – offers a list of such distinctly European values.

'Distinctly European' values? This qualification does not refer to the limits of their current or more importantly their potential *appeal* (which, this being again an integral trait of European identity, is presumed to be universal, all-human; the distinctive feature of European values is to believe that values 'make sense' only if seen as all-inclusive, and are indefensible unless applied to all humanity), but to their *origin*. These values are 'distinctly European' because they were thought out, articulated and refined in the part of the planet that tends to be described as 'Europe proper', and their articulation and refinement cannot be separated from the course of Europe's history. It was precisely by way of their articulation and refinement that the location and successive historical avatars of Europe took their course.

'Rationality' comes first on Todorov's list. Rationality, let me emphasize once and for all (and so save the need of repeating it when further values are discussed), as a *value*, not a feature of Europe's daily reality. By the criteria set by the value of 'rationality', Europe's past and present are strewn with acts of utter irrationality. Much of what happened and was done in Europe's history would not today pass a test of reason – and it hardly could, since what passed for reason and for its criteria kept changing over time together with Europe itself. But the belief that all habits and their breaches need to justify themselves in the court of reason was and remains one habit that Europe has hardly ever broken. That belief elevated argument and discussion above force – it was a prompt 'to exchange arguments more often than blows'.

'Really existing Europe' being always some way behind the Europe that Europe craved to be, that belief made Europeans inherently critical and self-critical. Seats in the supreme court could be reserved at all times for reason and reason alone – but no incumbents speaking in its name at any particular time were truly safe from critical scrutiny. We can say in retrospect that criticism and disaffection, rather than self-confidence and freedom from doubt, proved to be the most lasting contents of 'rationality' as a European value. To be rational, in the meaning which the idea of 'rationality' has been given or has acquired in European history, means never to be free from suspicion that the precepts of reason have been misread, or misunderstood, or misapplied – and that corrections are in order, urgently.

'Justice' is listed second on Todorov's list. Another value, let me comment, whose nature is best grasped as a pang of conscience, or through the metaphors of a thorn in the flesh, a spur, or yeast. The line separating the 'just' from the 'unjust' seldom stands still for long. It would be difficult and in all probability impossible to envisage a society in which further boundary corrections would be redundant and to hope that a particular description would command a consensus for long (though to expect that attempts to freeze the line will stop being made is similarly unwise). Like 'rationality', that shows its true power when it is turned against the currently pronounced verdicts of reason, 'justice' reveals its true might when the society of the day stands accused of unfairness, inequity, favouritism, corruption or bias. The closest one can come to a definition of a 'just society' is to say that society is 'just' when it does not believe itself to be just enough and is therefore determined to try harder.

Taking 'justice' as a value in its own right, as a non-instrumental value, casts all other values in a subsidiary, instrumental role. It offers justice at least a chance of immunity against the virus of seduction by other, more brightly glittering prizes. 'Justice' reminds us that there are other aims to think of, and that if they have been forgotten the time has come to pause and reflect. But there is more to justice's unique and irreplaceable role: in addition to being a judge, a trimmer and a corrector of all other values, whether embraced in passing or more obstinate, justice is also the one value that guards the *common* good (that is, from everyone's point of view, the good of others) against the inroads of egotistic self-promotion. It is a value that underlies all solidarity and thereby makes society possible. 'Justice' primes the human habitat for peaceful and friendly togetherness. It sets the table – a round table – for polylogue and negotiations guided by the will of agreement. Justice is the most 'socializing' of values. It may prompt the most frenzied confrontations, but in the end it unifies and heals the divisions; and as we know from Simmel, disagreement is the royal road to consensus. Exemption from the human family and consignment to waste may sometimes be a verdict of reason – but it would never be upheld in the court of justice.

Next on the list of Europe's foremost, indeed defining values is 'democracy'. As a value, democracy may beget and inform many fashions for going about the management and settlement of shared human affairs – many and different, sometimes sharply different. There are on the face of it more differences than similarities between the Athenian agora and the Reichstag, not to mention the Strasbourg gatherings. And yet there is a family resemblance that allows them all to be recognized as carriers of the same set of genes; as many and varied renditions of the same principles inspired by the same value.

What is that 'something' that unites them all? A feature which Cornelius Castoriadis singled out as the decisive constituent of 'autonomous society'[2] (as opposed to 'heteronomous societies', that is, those which 'incorporated in their institutions an idea not to be contested by their members: the idea that their institutions are not human-made, were not created by humans, at least not by humans who are alive at the moment', and therefore cannot be unmade or even reformed by the humans who are alive at the moment – as 'there is no alternative', the favourite excuse of present-day political actors, attempts, fortunately with limited effect, to suggest).

The essence of an autonomous society, the awareness that all its ways and means have only the will of its living members to rest on, has been embodied in the preamble with which the ancient Athenians preceded all laws voted in at the agora: 'edoxe te boule kai to demo', 'it is deemed good by the council and the people'. Several crucial assumptions were compressed in that formula, succinct yet saying it all: that there is something called 'good' which can be recognized as such; that choosing that good instead of its alternatives, not as good or no good at all, is the purpose of public deliberation preceding a decision; that discussion and argument leading to the decision is the way to make the right choice; and that when at the end of the day the choice has been made, everyone involved and affected by it needs to remember that the reason for making it was no more, but no less either, than that it was *deemed* good by the council and the people of the day. 'Deemed': that means that even if the council and the people tried hard to arrive at a joint decision in the light of their knowledge of what is good, that knowledge could be incomplete or downright erroneous. Debate is never finished; it can't be, lest democracy be no longer democratic and society be stripped of or forfeit its autonomy. Democracy means that the citizen's task is never complete. Democracy exists through persevering and unyielding citizens' concern. Once that concern is put to sleep, democracy expires.

And so there is not, and cannot be, a democracy, an autonomous society, without autonomous citizens – that is, citizens endowed with individual liberty and individual responsibility for the ways they use it. That liberty is another value – though unthinkable in separation from the value of democracy. Democracy rests on the freedom of its citizens, and citizens rest their confidence of being free and the courage to be free on the democracy of their *polis*. The two make each other and are made in the process of that making.

I suggest that it was the combination of all the named values that set Europe on its continuous, unfinished and hopefully unfinishable adventure. Mix those values together – and you get an inherently unstable compound, unlikely ever to solidify, constantly ready to interact with other substances, absorb or assimilate them; this is probably the quality of Europe which the theorists of 'reflexive modernity' wished to grasp and name, though they did it, like Minerva's owl, only when the phenomenon in question had fallen on hard times and faced, once Europe had lost its centuries-long role of the planetary pattern-setter, a genuine danger of premature termination.

And this is probably what prompted Lionel Jospin to invest his hopes in Europe on the grounds of its 'nuanced approach to current realities'.[3] Europe has learned, the hard way and at an enormous price paid in the currency of human suffering, 'how to get past historical antagonisms and peacefully resolve conflicts' and how to bring together 'a vast array of cultures' and to live with the prospect of permanent cultural diversity, no longer seen as only a temporary irritant. And note that these are precisely the sorts of lessons the rest of the world most badly needs. When seen against the background of the conflict-ridden planet, Europe looks like a laboratory where the tools necessary to construct Kant's Allgemeine Vereinigung der Menschheit ('universal unification of humanity') keep being designed, and like a workshop in which they keep being 'tested in action', though for the time being in the performance of less ambitious, smaller scale jobs. The tools that are currently being forged and put to the test inside Europe serve above all the delicate operation (for some observers too delicate for anything more than a sporting chance of success) of separating the bases of political legitimacy, democratic procedure and willingness for community-style sharing of assets from the principle of national/territorial sovereignty with which they have been, for most of modern history, inextricably linked.

In the nation-state, the wedlock of power and politics was defined and fixed *territorially*; the slow and twisted progress of an international *modus coexistendi* was aimed at corroborating and reinforcing that principle – leading eventually to the establishment of the United Nations, with a brief to protect the territorially confined sovereignty of states from outside aggression and interference. That marriage 'made in heaven' between politics and power, and their family household, the territorial nation-state, is, however, coming under assault nowadays from the outside and the inside simultaneously. For the emergent global powers, territorial political enclaves look ever more like so many 'rotten boroughs' holding back the integration of a new, vaster realm, while the indivisible right to decide the laws of the realm obstinately clung to by such nation-state enclaves feels increasingly similar to those

economically senseless and counterproductive local constraints (municipal, parish, landed) against which boister-
ous and vigorous entrepreneurs rebelled two centuries ago
when their eyes were set on larger (would-be national)
playing grounds.

The budding European federation is now facing the task
of repeating the feat accomplished by the nation-state of
early modernity: the task of bringing back together power
and politics, presently separated and navigating in opposite directions. The road leading to the implementation of
that task is as rocky now as it was then, strewn with snares
and spattered with incalculable risks. Worst of all, it is
unmapped, and each successive step seems like a leap
into the unknown.

Many observers doubt the wisdom of the endeavour and
give a low score to the chances of its success. The sceptics
don't believe in the viability of a 'postnational' democracy,
or any democratic political entity above the level of the
nation. They insist that allegiance to civic and political
norms would not replace 'ethno-cultural ties'[4] and that
citizenship is unworkable on a purely 'civilizational'
(legal-political) basis without the assistance of 'Eros' (the
'emotional dimension') – while assuming that 'ethno-
cultural ties' and 'Eros' are inextricably connected to the
kind of past-and-destiny-sharing sentiment which in history went under the name of nationalism: that allegiance to
those norms can strike roots and grow only inside this
connection and cannot be rebuilt or established anew in
any other way. The possibility that national legitimation of
state power was but a historically confined episode, one of
many alternative fashions of a reunion of politics and
power, or that the modern blend of statehood and nationhood bore more symptoms of a marriage of convenience
than of the verdict of providence or historical inevitability,
or that the marriage itself is not a foregone conclusion and,

when arranged, may be as stormy as most divorce procedures tend to be (as is vividly shown by the experience of the
post-colonial and post-empire artefactual political entities)
is thereby dismissed by the simple expedient of begging the
question.

Jürgen Habermas is arguably the most consistent and
the most authoritative spokesman for the point of view
opposite to that kind of scepticism. 'A democratic order
does not inherently need to be mentally rooted in "the
nation" as a pre-political community of shared destiny.
The strength of the democratic constitutional state lies
precisely in its ability to close the holes of social integration
through the political participation of its citizens.'[5] This is
true, but the issue goes further than that: 'the nation', as
any promoter of the 'national idea' would eagerly admit, is
as vulnerable and frail without a state that protects it
(indeed, assures its continuing identity) as the state is
without the nation that legitimizes its demands. Modern
nations and modern states are the twin products of the
same historical constellation. One might 'precede' the
other only in the short run, trying to make that short run
as short as possible and filling it with efforts to replace
priority with simultaneity and inserting an equation mark
between the ostensibly autonomous partners. The French
state was 'preceded' by Savoyards and Bretons, not
French people; the German state by Bavarians and Prussians, not Germans. Savoyards and Bretons would hardly
have turned into French and Bavarians and Prussians into
Germans were their reincarnation not 'power assisted' by,
respectively, the French and the German states.

For all practical intents and purposes, modern nations
and modern states alike emerged in the course of simultaneous and closely intertwined processes of nation and
state building; anything but cloudless processes, and anything but guaranteed to succeed. To say that a political

framework cannot be established without a viable ethno-cultural organism already in place is neither more nor less convincing than to say that no ethno-cultural organism is likely to become and stay viable without a working and workable political framework. A chicken-and-egg dilemma if there ever was one.

Habermas's comprehensive and grinding analysis points in a very similar direction:

> precisely the artificial conditions in which national con-sciousness arose argue against the defeatist assumption that a form of civic solidarity among strangers can only be generated within the confines of the nation. If this form of collective identity was due to a highly abstractive leap from the local and dynastic to national and then to demo-cratic consciousness, why shouldn't this learning process be able to continue?[6]

Shared nationhood is not a *necessary* condition of the legitimacy of the state authority if the state is a genuinely democratic body: 'The citizens of a democratic legal state understand themselves as the authors of the law, which compels them to obedience as its addressees.'[7] We may say that nationalism fills the legitimation void left (or unfilled in the first place) by the democratic participation of citi-zens. It is in the *absence* of such participation that an invocation of nationalist sentiments and efforts to beef them up are the state's sole recourse. The state must build its authority on the willingness of its subjects to die for the country if and when the country seems to need its residents solely for their readiness to sacrifice their lives and can well do without their contribution to the daily running of its affairs.

The detractors of the 'European project' dismiss the hope for a supranational 'European identity', asking 'who would wish to die for Javier Solana?' (or Romano Prodi, for that matter). What they prudently refrain from asking is how many people would wish to give their lives for Jacques Chirac, Gerhard Schröder, Tony Blair, George or George W. Bush, or even Jean-Marie Le Pen. Asking that other question would defy their purpose, as it would disclose the futility of their argument, making it obvious just how outdated and irrelevant to the prospect of European unity the first question was.

The 'heroic patriotism' to which that first question refers, and which it tacitly assumes to be still a plausible proposition, is clearly *passé*; it is neither on offer nor in demand. Just how far out of tune it is with the present condition of Europe is shown in the way that we (people born and bred on a continent strewn with the graves of 'unknown soldiers' and monuments to the glory of other martyrs who gave their lives for king and country) are unable to comprehend, let alone to approve, the motives that can prompt young, often highly educated men and women from other parts of the world to turn into suicide bombers, giving their lives 'to the cause'. Baffled, we try to understand their behaviour in a fashion that better suits our own thoughts and feelings: by the posthumous consumer delights deceitfully promised by the agents of exotic religious creeds. Such an explanation sounds much more credible to us than giving one's life to God or nation.

Just as Protestant ethics played the role of 'vanishing mediator' to an emergent modern capitalism, and lost its function and grip once its job had been done and it was no longer needed by a self-reliant capitalism, 'heroic patriotism' assisted the birth and maturation of the modern nation-state and then wilted and faded away once that state found less taxing ways to sustain its continuous existence than beefing up the emotions of the popular masses. An inclination to resort to the strategies of the last victorious war is a weakness that politicians share with the generals; but whether a repetition of the power-assisted 'spiritual mobilization' of the nation-and-state-building era will be a necessary condition of raising loyalties to the continental level is an open question and by no means a foregone conclusion. The European Union will not be and cannot be an enlarged copy of a nation-state, just as nation-states were not and could not be bigger versions of estates, parishes or municipalities. Anyone who takes a willingness to die for Javier Solana as the test of the feasibility and viability of the European Union mistakes the final product of a long nation-building process for a preliminary condition of all social integration at a higher level.

The sentiments of shared belonging and of mutual responsibility for the shared future, the willingness to care for each other's well-being and to find amicable and durable solutions to sporadically inflamed conflicts – all those features of common life compressed for a large part of the modern era into the idea of 'nationhood' – *necessarily* need an institutional framework of opinion- and will-formation, currently compressed in the idea of a democratically run sovereign state. The European Union is aiming, however slowly and haltingly, towards a rudimentary (or embryonic – the future will decide which of the two concepts fits better) form of such state, encountering on its way as the most obtrusive obstacles the existing nation-states and their reluctance to part with whatever is left of their once fully fledged sovereignty. The current direction is difficult to plot unambiguously, and prognosticating its future twists and turns is even more difficult (in addition to being irresponsible and unwise). The present momentum is shaped by two different (perhaps complementary, but then perhaps incompatible) logics – and it is impossible to decide, pre-empting history, which logic will ultimately prevail. One is the *logic of local retrenchment*; the other is the *logic of global responsibility and global aspiration*.

The first logic is that of the quantitative expansion of the territory-and-resource basis for the *Standortkonkurrenz* strategy. Even if no attempts had ever been made by the founders of the European Common Market and their successors to emancipate economies from their relatively incapacitating confinement in the *Nationalökonomie* framework, the 'war of liberation' currently conducted by capital, finance and trade enterprise against 'local constraints', a war triggered and intensified not by local interests but by global departures, would anyway be waged and go on unabated. The role of European institutions *does not* consist in eroding the sovereignty of member states and in particular in exempting economic activity from their controlling (and constraining) interference; in short, not in facilitating, let alone initiating, the divorce procedure between power and politics. For this purpose, the services of the European institutions are hardly required. Their function consists, on the contrary, in *stemming the tide*: arresting the capital assets that have escaped from the cages of the nation-state inside the continental stockade and keeping them there. If the effective enclosure of the capital, financial, commodity and labour markets and the balancing of books inside a single nation-state become ever more daunting tasks in view of the rising might of global capital, perhaps severally, or all together, the combined powers of nation-states will be able to match and confront it on more equal terms? In other words, the logic of local entrenchment is that of reconstructing at the Union level the legal-institutional web which in the past held together the 'national economy' within the boundaries of a nation-state's territorial sovereignty – but no longer does. But, as Habermas puts it, 'the creation of larger political unities in itself changes nothing about the mode of locational competition as such.'[8] Viewed from a planetary perspective, the joint strategy of a continental combination of states is hardly distinguishable from the codes of conduct of single nation-states which it came to replace. It is still guided by the logic of division, separation and enclosure – of seeking territorial exemptions from general rules and trends, local solutions for globally generated problems.

The logic of global responsibility on the other hand (and once that responsibility is acknowledged and taken, also of global aspiration) is aimed, at least in principle, at confronting globally generated problems point-blank – at their own level. It stems from the assumption that lasting and truly effective solutions to the planet-wide problems can only be found and only work through the renegotiation and reform of the web of global interdependencies and interactions. Instead of just aiming at the least local damage and the most local benefits to be derived from the capricious and haphazard drifts of global economic forces, it prefers to pursue a new kind of global setting, in which the paths of economic initiatives anywhere on the planet will no longer be whimsical and guided by momentary gains alone, with no attention paid to side-effects and 'collateral casualties', and no importance attached to the social dimensions of cost-and-effects balances. In short, that logic is aimed, to quote Habermas again, at the development of 'politics that can catch up with global markets'.[9]

Unlike the logic of local entrenchment, which mostly replays the persistent tunes of the raison d'état philosophy universally (or almost) dominant in the era of the nation-state, the logic of global responsibility and aspirations ushers us into unknown territory and opens up an era of political experimentation. It rejects the road of local defence against planetary trends as a known blind alley; it abstains (by necessity if not by reasons of conscience) from falling back on the orthodox European strategy of treating planetary space as a 'hinterland' on to which problems home-produced yet not capable of being resolved at home can be unloaded. It accepts that it would be utterly point-less to follow the first option with a realistic hope of even a modicum of success; whereas – having lost its global dom-ination and living instead in the shadow of a new planetary empire it can try at best to contain and mitigate, but hardly to control – Europe is not in a position to follow the second option, however successful that course might have been in the past and however tempting it still may be.

And so, willy-nilly, new unexplored strategies and tactics must be sought and tried, without the possibility of reliably calculating, let alone assuring, ultimate success. 'At the global level', Habermas warns, 'coordination prob-lems that are already difficult at the European level grow still sharper.' This is because 'civic solidarity is rooted in particular collective identities', whereas 'cosmopolitan solidarity has to support itself on the moral universalism of human rights alone', while the 'political culture of a world society lacks the common ethical-political dimen-sion that would be necessary for a corresponding global community.'[10]

A genuine 'Catch 22': the community which could underlie a common ethical sensibility and make political coordination feasible, thus providing the necessary condi-tion that must be met if supranational and supracontinen-tal (indeed, supracivilizational) solidarity is to sprout and take root, is difficult to attain precisely because the 'eth-ical-political dimension' is thus far missing and is likely to go on being missing, or to stop short of what is needed, as long as the community is incomplete. What Europe faces now is the prospect of developing, gradually and *simultan-eously*, and possibly through a long series of trials and errors, its objectives *and* the tools fit to tackle and resolve them (Jacques Delors called today's Europe a 'UPO' – an unidentified political object . . . ). To make the task yet more daunting, the ultimate destination of all that labour, an effective planetary policy based on a continuous poly-logue rather than on a planetary government, is equally unprecedented. Only historical practice may prove (though never disprove) its feasibility; or, more correctly, *render* it feasible.

We feel, guess, suspect what needs to be done. But we cannot know in what shape or form it will eventually happen. We can be pretty sure though, that the shape will not be familiar – it will be different from everything we've got used to. The political institutions at our disposal now were made to the measure of the territorial sover-eignty of the nation-state; they resist being stretched, and the political institutions that will serve the self-constitution of the planet-wide human community won't be, can't be, 'the same, only bigger'. We may well sense that the passage from 'international' agencies and tools of action to 'universal' institutions for all humanity has to be a qualita-tive, not merely a quantitative change. So we may ponder, and worry, whether the frames of 'global politics' presently available can accommodate (indeed, serve as an incubator for) the practices of the emergent global polity. What about the United Nations, for instance – briefed at its birth to guard and defend the undivided sovereignty of the state over its territory? What about the binding force of global laws – can it depend on the (revocable!) agree-ment of a sovereign member of the 'international commu-nity' to be obeyed?

To grasp the logic of the fateful departures in seven-teenth-century European thought, Reinhardt Kosseleck deployed the trope of the 'mountain pass'. It is indeed a felicitous metaphor once more, for us as we struggle to anticipate the twists and turns which the twenty-first cen-tury will inevitably bring in its course, and for future histor-ians as they pen their accounts retrospectively defining it.

Like our ancestors three centuries ago, we are on a rising slope of a mountain pass we have never climbed before and so have no inkling of what sort of a view will open up once we reach the top. We are not sure where the twisting gorge will lead us; one thing we are sure of is that we cannot settle and rest here, on a steeply rising path. And so we move on 'because'; because we can't stand still for long. Only when (if) we reach the top of the pass and survey the landscape on its other side will the time come to move 'in order to'; pulled rather than pushed, and pulled ahead by visions, purposes and chosen destinations.

For the time being, little can be said of that vexingly distant time except that it will (hopefully) arrive; that is, if there are still climbers left to find out that it has, and to say so. I suggested that much to Kosseleck, pointing to the rarity of prophetic talents and the notorious deficiencies of scientific prediction. In his reply, however, Kosseleck added an argument that was yet more decisive: we don't even have the concepts in which to couch our anticipation. Such concepts are formed in the practice of climbing, and not a moment before. Of the other side of the mountain pass, prudent climbers ought to keep silent.

This does not mean that the climbers should stop going on. And in the case of Europeans, known for their fondness for adventure and knack for experimentation, it is unlikely that they will. There will be a need for many stark choices, all made under conditions of severely limited knowledge (this is exactly what sets an adventure apart from routine and acting on command). The adverse odds seem truly daunting, but there are also hopes that are anything but empty, that are rooted firmly in the daily life of Europeans and are even more redoubtably manifest in moments of crisis.

In a conversation held in May 2003, Jürgen Habermas and Jacques Derrida called 15 February 2003 'another fourth of July' but this time on an all-European scale: the day on which 'a genuine shared European conscience' was born.[11] On that day, millions of Europeans went out into the streets of Rome, Madrid, Paris, Berlin, London and other capitals of Europe to manifest their unanimous condemnation of the invasion of Iraq about to be launched – and show obliquely their shared historical memory of past sufferings and a shared revulsion towards violence and atrocities committed in the name of national rivalries.

Madeleine Bunting thanks Spain 'for giving us a choice' after the terrorist bombs in Madrid, and the new government's decision to withdraw Spain's soldiers in Iraq, a choice between politicians who know mostly how to promise the frightened and the confused a 'wrathful vengeance' and more blood to be shed, and 'the Spanish woman who said she had felt no hate, only sadness'.[12] The politicians, Bunting suggests, 'would do well to listen, and articulate their civility rather than rush to use the shabby and meaningless metaphor of a "war on terror" . . . You cannot fight fire with fire, was the implicit message of the silent crowds' on the streets of Spanish cities.

The choice is between our cities turning into places of terror 'where the stranger is to be feared and distrusted', or sustaining their legacy of mutual civility between citizens and 'solidarity of strangers', solidarity strengthened by emerging victorious from the hardest of tests.

The logic of global responsibility/aspiration, if adopted and given priority over the logic of local retrenchment, may help to prepare Europe for its prospective adventure, perhaps greater than all its previous ones. Despite the formidably adverse odds, it could once more cast Europe in the role of global pattern-setter; it may enable Europe to deploy its values and the political/ethical experience of democratic self-government it has acquired, in order to assist in the substitution of a fully inclusive, universal

human community for a collection of territorially entrenched entities engaged in a zero-sum game of survival. Only with the achievement of such a community
can Europe's mission be accomplished. Only within such
a community can the values enlightening Europe's
ambitions and pursuits be truly safe.

What lies ahead has been prophetically put into writing
by Franz Kafka[13] – as a premonition, a warning and an
encouragement:

> So if you find nothing in the corridors open the doors, if
> you find nothing behind these doors there are more floors,
> and if you find nothing up there, don't worry, just leap up
> another flight of stairs. As long as you don't stop climbing,
> the stairs won't end, under your climbing feet they will go
> on growing upwards.

# Notes

## Chapter 1    An Adventure called 'Europe'

1   Denis de Rougemont, 'L'aventure mondiale des Européens' (1962), in *Écrits sur l'Europe* (Éditions de la Différence, Paris, 1994).

2   Quoted after Cees Nooteboom, *L'Enlèvement d'Europe* (Calmann-Levy, Paris, 1994).

3   Alex Warleigh, *Democracy in the European Union: Theory, Practice and Reform* (Sage, London, 2003). See also V. Goddard, J. Llobera and C. Shore (eds), *The Anthropology of European Identity and Boundaries in Conflict* (Berg, Oxford, 1994); and Norman Davies, *Europe: A History* (Pimlico, London, 1997).

4   Hans-Georg Gadamer, *Das Erbe Europas* (1989), here quoted after *L'Héritage de l'Europe*, French trans. by Philippe Invernel (Rivage Poche, Paris, 1996), pp. 39–40.

5   See Krzysztof Pomian, 'Europe et ses frontières', in *L'Europe retrouvée* (Éditions de la Baconière, Neuchâtel, 1992).

6   See de Rougemont, 'L'aventure mondiale des Européens'.

7   See Gøran Therborn, 'Entangled modernities', *European Journal of Social Theory* (Aug. 2003).

8   See Eduardo Lourenço, 'De l'Europe comme culture', in *L'Europe introuvable* (Éditions Métailié, Paris, 1991).

9  Michel de Montaigne, *The Complete Essays*, trans. M. A. Screech (Penguin, Harmondsworth, 1991), p. 231.

10  See Wolf Lepenies, 'Koniec wieku Europy?' (The end of the European age?), in *Europa Wschodu i Zachodu* (Poznań, 1998).

11  Naomi Klein, 'Fortress continents', *Guardian*, 16 Jan. 2003, p. 23; first published in the *Nation*.

12  Jelle van Buuren, 'Les tentacules du système Schengen', in *Obsessions sécuritaires*, issue of *Manière de voir* 71 (2003), pp. 24–6.

13  Quoted after Alan Travis, 'Tough asylum policy "hits genuine refugees"', *Guardian*, 29 Aug. 2003, p. 11.

14  Couze Venn, 'World dis/order: on some fundamental questions', *Theory, Culture, Society* (Aug. 2002), pp. 121–36.

15  Antonia Juhasz, 'Capitalism gone wild', *Tikkun* 1 (2004), pp. 19–22.

16  Naomi Klein, 'America is not a hamburger', *Los Angeles Times*, 10 Mar. 2002; repr. in Klein, *Fences and Windows* (Flamingo, London, 2002).

17  See Naomi Klein, *No Logo* (Flamingo, London, 2001).

18  See Klein, *Fences and Windows*.

19  See Ryszard Kapuściński, *Lapidarium V* (Warsaw, 2002).

20  See Sheldon Rampton and John Stauber, 'Trading on fear', *Guardian Weekend*, 12 July 2003.

21  Joseph Stiglitz, 'Trade imbalances', *Guardian*, 15 Aug. 2003.

22  See 'L'ampleur des désaccords Nord-Sud met l'OMC en échec', *Le Monde*, 16 Sept. 2003, p. 2.

23  At www.europa-web.de/europa/02wwswww/203chart/chart_gb. htm (accessed Apr. 2004).

24  See Jürgen Habermas, *The Liberating Power of Symbols* (Polity, Cambridge, 2001).

25  V. Inozemtsev and E. Kuznetsova, 'European values and American interests', *International Affairs* 3 (2003), pp. 59–69.

26  Will Hutton, *The World We Are In* (Little, Brown, London, 2002), p. 370.

27  Ulrich K. Preuss, 'The Iraq war: critical reflections from "Old Europe"', *Constellations* 3 (2003), pp. 339–51.

28  Robert Kagan, 'Power and weakness', *Policy Review* (June–July 2002).

29  Étienne Balibar, 'Europe: vanishing mediator', *Constellations* 3 (2003), pp. 312–38.

30  Eugen Weber, 'The myth of the nation-state and the creation of the "other"', *Critical Review* 3–4 (2003), pp. 387–402.

31  Robert Fine, 'Taking the "ism" out of cosmopolitanism', *European Journal of Social Theory* 6 (2003), pp. 451–70.

32  See Richard Rorty, 'Globalization, the politics of identity and social hope', in Rorty, *Philosophy and Social Hope* (Penguin, Harmondsworth, 1999).

33  George Monbiot, 'With eyes wide shut', *Guardian*, 12 Aug. 2003.

34  See Zygmunt Bauman, *In Search of Politics* (Polity, Cambridge, 1999), and *Society under Siege* (Polity, Cambridge, 2002).

## Chapter 2   In the Empire's Shadow

1  Zbigniew Brzezinski, *The Grand Chessboard: American Primacy and its Geostrategic Imperatives* (Basic Books, New York, 1997), p. 24.

2  Henry Kissinger, *Does America Need a Foreign Policy? Toward a Diplomacy for the Twenty-First Century* (Simon and Schuster, New York, 2001), p. 17.

3  Joseph S. Nye Jr, *The Paradox of American Power* (Oxford University Press, Oxford, 2002), p. 1.

4  Robert Kagan, *Of Paradise and Power: America and Europe in the New World Order* (Knopf, New York, 2003), p. 26.

5  Michael Mann, *Incoherent Empire* (Verso, London, 2003), p. 13.

6  Ibid., p. 18.

7   Michael Ignatieff, 'The burden', *New York Times Magazine*, 5 Jan. 2002.
8   Tzvetan Todorov, *Le nouveau désordre mondiale* (Robert Laffont, Paris, 2003), p. 18.
9   Ibid., p. 20.
10  David Harvey, *The New Imperialism* (Oxford University Press, Oxford, 2003), pp. 23–5.
11  See John Pilger, 'What good friends left behind', *Guardian Weekend*, 20 Sept. 2003, pp. 43–9.
12  Benjamin R. Barber, *Fear's Empire; War, Terrorism, and Democracy* (W. W. Norton, New York, 2003), p. 17.
13  Jürgen Habermas, *The Postnational Constellation: Political Essays*, trans. Max Pensky (Polity, Cambridge, 2001), pp. 80, 61.
14  Polly Toynbee, 'The real reason why we should fear immigration', *Guardian*, 11 Feb. 2004, p. 20.
15  Rorty, 'Globalization, the politics of identity and social hope', p. 233.
16  Richard Rorty, 'Back to class politics', in Rorty, *Philosophy and Social Hope*, p. 258.
17  See Eric Leser, 'L'amertume des cols bleus', *Le Monde*, 16 Jan. 2004, p. 15,
18  Following data collated by A. Krueger ('Economic scene', *New York Times*, 3 Apr. 2003) and J. Madrick ('The Iraqi time bomb', *New York Times*, 6 Apr. 2003); see Harvey, *The New Imperialism*, p. 206.
19  In the State of the Union Address on 28 Jan. 2003.
20  Barber, *Fear's Empire*, p. 37.
21  Quoted after Mark Seddon, 'Bush and Blair promised justice in Iraq. Another lie', *Guardian*, 30 June 2003, p. 16.
22  In a book of interviews conducted by Giovanna Borradori, here quoted after the reprint in *Le Monde diplomatique*, Feb. 2004, p. 16, 'Qui est-ce que le terrorisme?'
23  Habermas, *The Postnational Constellation*, p. 17.
24  Barber, *Fear's Empire*, p. 30.
25  Ibid., p. 21.
26  Harvey, *The New Imperialism*, pp. 141–2.

27  Ibid., pp. 150–1.
28  R. Wade and F. Veneroso, 'The Asian crisis: the high debt model versus the Wall Street–Treasury–IMF complex', *New Left Review* 228 (1998), pp. 3–23,
29  Kagan, 'Power and weakness'.
30  Balibar, 'Europe'.
31  Harvey, *The New Imperialism*, pp. 16–17.
32  I have surveyed such factors in my *Work, Consumerism and the New Poor* (Open University Press, Buckingham, 1998; 2nd edn, 2004).
33  Allyson Pollock. 'Selling off by stealth is here to stay', *Guardian*, 11 Feb. 2004, p. 20.
34  Habermas, *The Postnational Constellation*, p. 112.
35  Ulrich Beck, *Risk Society: Towards a New Modernity*, trans. Mark Ritter (Sage, London, 1992), p. 75.
36  See my *Wasted Lives: Modernity and its Outcasts* (Polity, Cambridge, 2004), pp. 46–53.
37  See Balibar, 'Europe'.
38  Umberto Eco, *La Recherche de la langue parfaite dans la culture européenne*, (Seuil, Paris, 1994).

## Chapter 3  From Social State to Security State

1  See Franz Kafka, 'The burrow', here quoted from Willa and Edwin Muir's translation in *The Collected Stories of Franz Kafka*, ed. Nahum N. Glatzer (Penguin, Harmondsworth, 1988), pp. 325–59.
2  Robert Castel, *L'Insécurité sociale. Qu'est-ce qu'être protégé?* (Seuil, Paris, 2003), p. 5.
3  Sigmund Freud, *Civilization and its Discontents*, here quoted from the Penguin Freud Library edn, vol. 12, pp. 274 ff.
4  Castel, *L'insécurité sociale*, p. 6.
5  Ibid., p. 22.
6  Ibid., p. 46.
7  See my *Individualized Society* (Polity, Cambridge, 2002).

8   See Castel, *L'insécurité sociale*, pp. 47 ff.
9   Barber, *Fear's Empire*, pp. 158 ff.
10  Quoted after 'Asylum: a strategy emerges', *Guardian*, 25 Feb. 2004, p. 1.
11  See Alain Morice, 'L'Europe enterre le droit d'asile', *Le Monde diplomatique*, Mar. 2004, pp. 14–15.
12  'Une généalogie de l'insécurité contemporaine', entretien avec Philippe Robert, *Esprit*, Dec. 2002, pp. 35–58.
13  Richard Sennett, *The Corrosion of Character* (W. W. Norton, New York, 1998), p. 43.
14  Jacques Donzelot, 'Les nouvelles inégalités et la fragmentation territoriale', *Esprit*, Nov. 2003, pp. 132–57.
15  See my *Liquid Love* (Polity, Cambridge, 2003).
16  Weber, 'The myth of the nation-state'.
17  Jo Goodey, 'Whose insecurity? Organized crime, its victims and the EU', in *Crime and Insecurity: The Governance of Safety in Europe*, ed. Adam Crawford (Willan Publishing, Cullompton, Devon, 2002), pp. 136 ff.
18  Rory Carroll, 'In praise of smugglers', *Guardian*, 2 Sept. 2000, p. 8.

## Chapter 4   Towards a World Hospitable to Europe

1   See Todorov, *Le nouveau désordre mondial*, pp. 87ff.
2   Cornelius Castoriadis, 'L'individu privatisé', interview given to Robert Redeker in Toulouse, 22 Mar. 1997, reprinted in *Le Monde diplomatique*, Feb. 1998, p. 23.
3   See Lionel Jospin, 'Solidarity or playing solitaire', *Hedgehog Review* (spring 2003), pp. 32–44.
4   See, for instance, Cris Shore, 'Whither European citizenship?', *European Journal of Social Theory* (Feb. 2004), pp. 27–44.
5   Habermas, *The Postnational Constellation*, p. 76.
6   Ibid., p. 102.
7   Ibid., p. 101.
8   Ibid., p. 104.

9    Ibid., p. 109.

10   Ibid., pp. 104, 108.

11   See Jan-Werner Müller, 'Europe. Le pouvoir des sentiments: l'euro-patriotisme en question?', *La Vie des idées* (Apr.–May 2004), p. 19.

12   See Madeleine Bunting, 'Listen to the crowds', *Guardian*, 13 Mar. 2004, p. 21.

13   Franz Kafka, 'Advocates', trans. Tania Stern and James Stern, in *The Collected Short Stories of Franz Kafka*, p. 451.

# Index